Your First Year In Real Estate

Thomas Vargeletis

Introduction

This book provides an overview of the mistakes made by new real estate agents and methods used to correct them. When I started out I had no sales experience, no training, and no mentor. I had basically made every mistake that a new agent can make, and I had no other significant source of income to support my venture. My first year was a complete failure that found me on the brink of bankruptcy. Unfortunately, I didn't have a complete enough understanding of what I was getting myself into, and my motivation for getting started was somewhat misguided. I have been fortunate enough to rectify my situation after making some important changes. I even found the work rewarding after a while, but only through a financially stressful period of trial and error.

Like any industry, things are not always what they seem from the outside. If You're only beginning your career as an agent, or you have just been thinking about signing up for the class and getting you license, this book is for you. Few incoming agents are fully aware of the various and sundry niche markets, ancillary services and skills needed, and all of the work that actually goes in to being a real estate agent. I know that was true for me. There are a very few that enter this field knowing exactly what to do, and how to do it. Even fewer have a tight enough handle on their personal finances and budget so they can carry themselves through a bear market without much risk for losing everything. This book is the culmination of all of those painful lessons I had to learn in order to survive financially. I am presenting those lessons here so you don't have to make the same mistakes.

My knowledge of real estate before I had gotten my license I was marginal at best. I did not understand the important duties of an agent. Like many people on the outside looking in, I figured it was just a fun way to make easy money. One of the first important lessons I had learned there was no such thing as easy money! Over a short period of time, it became clear that I was in over my head. Every expectation that I had set before going into this field was either changed, or never met, at first. If I had known more, or had a mentor, or even had some basic resources to help me really understand the industry, I may have had a better start. However, if I had known everything about the job before I started, I might never have gotten licensed in the first place. I figured I was going to make the easiest paychecks of my life, and that was just not the case. After I got into the swing of things and started closing deals, I did finally start enjoying my work.

Why This Book is Important

This book is going to help someone who may be on the fence about getting started in real estate by providing insight into your day-to-day tasks and activities, and of the scope of work and responsibility involved with being an agent. The book is also going to help the new agent stay out of trouble, and give them some important tips on what to do and what not to do, especially if this is their first time in an industry where everyone is their own boss. This will provide homebuyers and sellers a great idea of what kinds of obstacles their agents have to overcome every day, and can help them form an opinion of what they are looking for when hiring an agent. This will be a great refresher for seasoned agents, and perhaps serve as a nostalgic reminder of past struggles.

I was an agent without a mentor, without previous sales experience, and without any reasonable idea of how I was supposed to make a living selling real estate. The best way to learn anything new is to surround yourself with the information you need. The higher quality of information, the better your learning and execution. This will create a rich and immersive learning experience. The best agents know this, and they are spending hours and hours learning, researching, and training.

Some of the knowledge presented here you may be already aware of. You may even have some experience with certain aspects of the work you are or will be doing, or maybe you are going in completely cold like I did. At any skill level, it is more important that you keep learning, and keep growing. At worst, if you study on your own, and learn on the job in your office or community, you might only take a couple tips that end up helping in some small way. The more knowledge we build up over time, the better our performance will be. That knowledge base is grown with material like this.

You will learn much in your first year as an agent. All I had was a very basic understanding of what real estate agents do from watching TV shows, and some quick research online. I also had a fairly pleasant experience when buying my first home, and as I was reading through the closing documents disclosing commission, I was amazed! I could not believe that he had been paid so much money, for what seemed like very little work. I was already someone with an interest and appreciation of the idea of real estate. When I saw that commission disclosure, I was thinking "Hey this is definitely for me!"

Not long after my first home purchase I was laid off from my job, and I knew I needed to find work and make some money fast. There was no other option in my mind except to become one of those millionaire agents. I took the class, passed the test, and tried to prepare myself for the unending fountain of riches. Now, in my first four months I closed over $1 million in business. That means, the total sum of sales prices from all of the closings was over a million. I had finally made it! I felt like I was one of those millionaire agents in those first months. At least, that's how I was spending my money.

For the next eight months, I didn't make a cent. Coming from a government job, I was used to money coming in automatically every fifteen days. Foolishly, my only limit on spending was my paycheck. with those first few checks I was making considerably more than I had before, so then I was spending more. Not many people are so ridiculous, but I made some bad financial decisions. I bought myself and my fiancé new cars (with loans), I bought us a sauna, a high end espresso machine, designer suits, jewelry, computer, smart watches, a pool table, the deluxe set of Cutco knives (worth more than a few mortgage payments), brand new appliances for the house, surround sound system for my pool table room, cordless blinds (well over $200 per window on my many, many windowed house), brand new furniture (handmade in the U.S.A., with U.S. wood), you name it and I ran out and threw money at it, as hard as I could.

If anyone were to tell me now that I had a spending problem, I think I would have to agree. I was living this idea of a high life that I assumed all real estate agents had. I thought I had figured out some magical secret that only a select few geniuses like me could enjoy. Remember, I had entered a new profession with no mentor, and no training. I had been relatively good at managing my own finances up until then, and I had never imagined that I would need to project my income far into the future instead of just that week.

I lived a dream for about four months, and then reality came knocking. I did not have one lead and no prospects for more business. I had no idea that I just closed what would be my last deal of the year, and I wouldn't realize it until it was far too late. I eventually got to the point where I was paying bills and buying food with credit cards. That experience was exactly as stressful and unsustainable as you can imagine. I would never have thought something like that could happen to me. In fact, the only way that I could find to turn that negative experience into a positive, is by using my experiences to tell new agents how to get started, and avoid that kind of stress all together.

Takeaways

I did not make the slightest effort to prepare myself for my new journey. I want to take those hard lessons learned in my first year, and present them for any new agents who may be having a sub par experience. My experiences should give those who are on the fence about deciding whether they should start working or not before they risk a large and potentially hazardous investment of time and money. This will help new agents guard against rookie mistakes I made, and set themselves up for success in the long run. I don't want to imply that every new agent out there that can't save money or make sound decisions. In fact, I am counting on them being much smarter than I was, especially since I have not met another soul who got a taste of cash and went on a spending frenzy. As much can be said for anyone picking up this book. I did not make the slightest effort to prepare myself for my new journey, and I paid dearly. I paid with more than just money. The stress of knowing that the only way you can buy food for your family is on credit is unbearable. If you want to give yourself the best chance, you will need full immersion into the real estate industry. You need books like this, you need to find a good mentor, and you need to commit to the necessary time and action that it will take to build your business. It will help you learn and develop your own ideas, and even help steer into other areas of important study. This book will help you guard against foolish and unproductive behavior no matter how large or small, and it will help you understand what you can do to make it through your most challenging year.

What Being An Agent Is All About

Recognition

One thing we all see from time to time are agents with some local celebrity. We even may see agents with national awards, or even TV shows. Real estate is not a very easy profession to break into as a beginner, partly because of the top performers who are constantly working to dominate their marketplace. Some agents always seem to stand out above the crowd. This special recognition may have inspired some new agents into joining the industry in the first place.

Being recognized feels great because all of that hard work has finally "paid off." Agents who work hard, and are dedicated to building their business are the ones who earn awards. Think about it like this: the real estate agent is the founder and CEO of their very own small business. Their products and inventory are the listings for sale on the market. Few agents can afford to hire help right away. That is because an agent isn't just an agent, they are also their own administrator, marketer, bookkeeper, document controller, driver, for sale sign planter, home stager/photographer, and on and on. Some companies will provide one of more of these services to their agents, but the rest is still on them. To juggle all of these tasks and still come out as a top producer can be time consuming and requires extraordinary organizational skills. Recognition and celebrity is a byproduct of building a great business, although it's a worthy goal to aspire for.

Professionalism

Real estate agents are professionals in the real estate industry. Not everybody in the industry is an agent. There are lawyers, home inspectors, contractors, appraisers, interior designers, movers, marketing/media companies, mortgage officers and many more. There is a difference between a professional and a non-professional. The pro's know their market, present well, and never cut corners. Professionals provide excellent service. This gives them credibility, esteem, and authority with clients. Non-pro's get the opposite. The agents who don't take their work seriously, who don't deliver perfect presentations lose credibility and income. All agents should aspire to be a professional.

Professionalism is in the perception. Any clients you work with will have certain expectations about you that must be met in their mind in order for your work to be appreciated. Does that mean that you can just fake it? No. Unfortunately, in this and many other industries, seeing is believing. Knowledge alone is not enough. Professionals needs to be knowledgeable, responsive and honest. They need to be faithful to their clients. There are a lot of factors that go into this, and luckily they are all relative. Like I said, you don't need to be the greatest agent in the world to make a great living, you don't need to be the best dressed ever, or have a presentation that brings tears to your client's eyes. You only need to meet your clients expectations, and sometimes exceed them for extra points. What are those expectations? Ask yourself, what do you think a professional is? Who is a professional, and how to they act, what do they look like? If you are selling a 12,000 square foot mansion by the sea, you are going to need to fit extremely high expectations. If you want to sell luxury real estate, you can't show up looking like you just came from your part-time job at Jiffy Lube. In fact, your bespoke suit could hurt your chances of earning business if you are ridiculously over-dressed for the occasion.

Depending on where you are and who you talk to, the definition of "professional" changes. When it comes to your appearance, dress-to-impress, but don't overdo it. Agents need to be professionals for everyone they are working with. In order to fully meet your client's expectations you need to pander a little. For example, what will some blue-collar workers meeting you at their humble abode in the country think about your formal presentation? They won't want to work with you. That happened to me once, and luckily it only had to happen once in order for the message to get through. I was getting ready for a listing presentation in a neighborhood that was populated mostly with workers at a nearby factory. They were honest and hard-working people, their lifestyle was very casual; they especially did not appreciate anyone who looked down on them, or someone who seemed to look down on them. I showed up in a fine designer suit (one of those unscrupulous wardrobe purchases), and instantly regretted it. My prospective client was instantly and obviously uncomfortable at the sight of me. If I was visiting a $1 million listing or just in a place where their were more people wearing suits, it would have been fine. My appearance was off-putting in that context. They thought I was an outsider, that I was some rich guy trying to take advantage of them. That prospect never called me back, or bothered to answer follow-up calls. The best part: they were worth a whole lot more money than me at the time.

On the other end of this spectrum, when I was an especially brand new agent, my broker would let me run an open house from time to time. I was showing a million dollar listing in an affluent area. I showed up in embarrassingly casual dress, perfectly provincial behavior to boot. I thought I was being friendly and welcoming, but my ideas of a friendly agent and theirs were different. Very early into the open house I realized to my extremely red-faced embarrassment that most of the attendees were not pleased with me. Some of the people had made polite attempts to aske me to go away. A couple others asked me with full sincerity if I knew where the Realtor was.

Buyers and sellers want to know that they are working with a professional, a market expert. Your behavior and appearance need to be as formal as your clients would expect. Buying and selling a home is often the largest transaction that most people will make in their lifetime. Buyers and sellers want to work with an agent who they feel is more than up to the task. Professionalism is equal parts form and substance. Market knowledge isn't enough by itself. Expensive clothing isn't proof that you are good at anything more than being a consumer. A well rounded professional has deep knowledge of their market, a professional appearance that fits the client's expectation, and is able to both educate their clients when necessary and articulate their value.

Community

Another way to help you succeed during your first year in business is getting involved in the community. If you participate in community events as a helping hand or an organizer/leader, you are meeting people, making business connections, and learning about the nuances in your community. Some of those new contacts will need your services soon, and the rest know someone who will. No houses can be sold without the people buying and selling them. Meeting business owners, other agents or real estate professionals, as well as simply making new friends will grow your network, and your income.

Community involvement is also part of becoming a market expert. Great agents are not just learning about the properties for sale in the area, but also about the lifestyle and other intangibles. Firsthand knowledge of your market will empower you to speak with certainty and authority about it. If you are already an active community member, then you are on the right track. New agents who have already been involved in some local events should use their latest career as an opportunity to expand the horizons of their present commitments. If you are a member at the historical society, don't stop there, join another group. Your sphere of influence is all of the people that you know, and if you are starting from 0, or if you are a town board member and a business owner, you can always afford just a little more time to make new connections. As you meet more and more people, you will have a warm network that you can reach out to and ask for business. Don't hold back from letting people know that you are now a real estate agent. That said, it wouldn't be a good idea to tactlessly shove your card into people's hands and demand a real estate transaction right when you meet them. There are agents who behave like this, and they are soon forgotten. Be unforgettable by caring about your new acquaintances, and nurture each new connection that you can.

know your market

While getting involved in the community is important, it also is a very wise business to decision to get to know the ins and outs of the community. During my first year, I felt that in order to do well financially, I needed to concentrate on listing and selling $1 million properties. A sound idea, its true that my commission on a million dollar home is higher than a million dime home. Unfortunately, I only learned half of the lesson. I was spending a lot of time looking at real estate in affluent communities, with almost no results! My problem? I didn't know the market, I didn't know the neighborhoods, I didn't know the people, schools, or anything else. Like the amateur I was, I didn't give those details very much attention. In fact, I gave them no attention at all. The essence of growing a real estate business is through developing personal relationships, and knowing your market. If you don't know the people, and you don't know the community, you won't get anywhere.

The nuances of a neighborhood and town do matter to buyers. Of course, someone would be wise to learn as many details as possible when they may possibly live there for the rest of their lives. What rational mind would want to risk spending hundreds of thousands of dollars on real estate in a town or neighborhood that they may not like? Some due diligence must be done. How can anyone know whether they will like a community or not? Sometimes the singular motivation for a buyer's interest in a town is because of what the community has to offer. Many families like to move for schools, parks, businesses, etc.. I was working hard to find buyers and sellers in affluent neighborhoods, which I'm sure I could have gotten an "A" for effort, but my bank account doesn't fill itself for wasted time. The few people that I did have an opportunity to meet and talk real estate with didn't feel very comfortable working with an agent who didn't know something about the town nor seem to care. How many people want to buy a house from an agent who could literally not answer one question they had? You guessed it, zero. Buyers and sellers want to work with someone who knows the area they are interested in, that's one of the most valuable skills a real estate agent has. A new agent must take advantage of their time and their tools to become that active community member. Buyers want to rest assured that no one else could find a better location for them to focus their home search in. Sellers want to know that no listing agent could better market their property and bring the right buyer because the agent understands the community. In my first year, I was not a community member, and I paid for it in lost business.

The lesson learned is new agents need to be prepared if they are targeting a specific community. Because I did not know the $1 million market that well, I gravitated back to cities that I had personally lived in, or had other close ties to. It turned out that I did know a market very well. That market was where clients were happy and comfortable to work with me. Just knowing the area, community, and all of those little things that make the city or town special helped my business immensely. It took more than a year to Learn that lesson, but I got there eventually.

Helping Others

Selling real estate is a service. You are helping an owner sell their home. You are helping a buyer purchase a property. These clients will need to move for all kinds of reasons. The very nature of you job as an agent is to help them make that move happen. At first, I figured that selling real estate was like running your own private mint. But if you are only hungry for income, your clients can sense it. If your clients feel like you are just trying to get paid, if they do not believe that you are looking out for their best interests, they are not going to be happy. An agent's work is service based, so the focus needs to be on providing that service at the highest quality. Agents need to care about their clients needs. When your clients needs are met, they will be content with the service. At a higher level, focus on helping your clients find their next home, gain their bearings in unfamiliar territory, and get the best deal possible. Far beyond merely showing a few houses and making a commission, if your service is outstanding, you will turn clients into advocates, and will earn their family and friends business thanks to word-of-mouth referrals.

It is important to hold your clients' needs clearly in your mind. Whether you think the same things are important or not, you will need to recognize that if your clients' expectations are not met, they will not have a positive experience. This kind of care will shine when you are finding absolutely perfect homes to show your buyers, and when you never skip a beat with representing your sellers interests. The more you are emotionally involved and attached to the outcome, the less mistakes you will make. If you are motivated by helping clients, you will pay more attention to the process and go above and beyond expectations to get the job done. This wont only help your buyers find their next home faster, or get better terms for your sellers. Taking this approach will turn your client into an advocate, and possibly pave the way for a lifetime of referrals. Great agents go far when they care, and it shows.

Personal Growth

When we talk about personal growth, we are simply talking about the development of your mindset and behavior over time. As we learn new things, and improve ourselves, we are growing. The wrong ideas about personal development can hurt your business development. It is important to focus on constantly improving, even if it is only in small ways. When I was first taking my real estate license class, I assumed that the material covered was going to fully prepare me for making all of those millions in real estate. Upon receiving my License, I felt that I already knew everything I needed to succeed. Obviously that was not the case. As I was dealing with the shell-shock of my failures I realized a few things. I learned that I was not only very far away from being the superstar of my imagination, my journey to success was going to be lifelong. Like in any career, there is a learning curve over time. As we gain more experience in our industry, our perception of our industry gains altitude. With a higher altitude of perception we can see a bigger picture than we once did. You could say the learning curve is skewed to the more formative years where you are learning much more thanks to the experience still being new. The first year is likely to be the most intense and enriching of them all, especially for new agents diving in head-first without a strong sales background. You will learn even more about your profession over the years. As a seasoned agent, you can still pick up a new trick or two. After years in the business, you may even refresh old ideas in a new way. Over your lifetime you will hone your skills, discipline, and more. Unless your life plan is to reach some point of mediocrity, you need to constantly learn and grow in your business and in your personal life. Making a habit of reading about real estate and sales, writing about it, going to conferences, and training. Maintain a mindset of constant learning and growth. The first year will teach you the most, but don't let the learning and your development end there. What happens when you find yourself more financially stable, and don't need to hustle quite as much? Do you lose your edge and let all of your momentum slip? What will you do when your priorities or other obligations change? Our lives are fluid, and in order to maintain steady and net positive growth, we have to make a habit of learning.

My biggest mistake is that I was convinced that I had all of the tools I needed to succeed. I assumed that I was already doing the right things and didn't take the time to study and improve myself. Whenever there was an unexpected demand on my time or vast fields of empty squares on my calendar, I wasted my time. If I had a whole day or two ahead with no appointments, instead of focusing on learning how to better generate leads, or doing anything productive, I treated the empty space like a mini vacation. I had to learn this lesson the hard way: If I do not take responsibility for my personal development, no one else will. At the time I was shocked to realize that my original self-assessment of being all-knowing and all-wise was wrong. I wasn't only second guessing my new career as I faced financial obliteration, I was second guessing every decision I had ever made. I thought that I was fully prepared to enter into the real estate world with no experience, no sales background or training, and no initiative to train and develop my (at that time) nonexistent real estate skills. If I had bothered to focus on self improvement for a moment, to try to learn more about the industry, and how to make myself a more effective human being, I would not have put myself in that situation. For the person who is constantly learning and growing, it's no big deal. If you are constantly in a self-aware state of learning, you can realize an error far before it devastates your business, pivot away from what isn't working, and put your attention and your action onto effective income generating activity. No real estate agent, no person in any industry, can afford to lose business thanks to bad habits or ineffective actions. Being a great agent means that you will also be a great student.

Teaching & Sharing

A real estate agent is also a real estate educator. In a world with so much information flying around, it can be impossible for clients to take the time to fully educate themselves on the process of buying or selling their home. When you sit down with a buyer or seller for the first time, they usually don't know much about the real estate industry, unless they have bought and sold property regularly. You will also meet clients who were or are real estate professionals in one form or another, and sometimes they will know more than you. However it is more likely that you are going to work with clients who don't know the industry very well.

Working with clients who are not familiar with the industry gives you a special opportunity to do two things. First, you have an opportunity to teach them about the business and help them understand the buying/selling process. Second, you get to reinforce your own knowledge through that act of teaching. Real estate, buyers (and sellers) are all intrinsically unique, and every deal is different. This always brings an opportunity to learn something new, or reinforce some old ideas. Your client's will have questions that you are unprepared for, or have no previous experience in. Being in a position where you will need to educate clients can test your knowledge. There is always a question that you had not thought of. Over time, the same issues will continue coming up, and you will have the benefit of repetition over time to help engrain the information into your psyche. Buyers not fully understanding the importance of getting a pre-approval/proof of funds before they start looking. Seller's expecting that a buyer won't notice some issue that they don't personally care about. Home inspector's pointing out certain problems that aren't all that bad in the end, but the buyers feel like it's a deal breaker. Certain questions and concerns that are frequently voiced will create a teachable moment with your clients. This teachable moment is your time to shine by showing that you really do know what you are doing. A new agent should take extra care with learning their work in order to avoid misrepresenting anything. Never, ever, ever make something up on the fly. If you are unprepared, you are unprepared, the only things you can say are: "I'm not exactly sure about this, and I don't want to give you the wrong information. I'll look into this and get back to you." Being ready for those common questions is easier than it may seem at first. Go to your fellow real estate agent's, and ask them, "what are the most common questions that you get from buyers/ sellers? "What kinds of problems or issues always come up when you are showing properties?" The idea is to draw information from your network. The knowledge and experience of other agents is usually available for the asking.

Just as important as learning about questions and other opportunities to help educate your clients, you don't want to misinform them. I've had the misfortune of boldly stating certain facts, and daring anyone to tell me I was wrong. I heard this one tidbit once, and that was it, but no one could ever crack my unshakeable foundation in that information. It was as fact as fact could be. One day as I was sitting in a continuing ed class, and an attorney teaching the class was casually explaining how very wrong I was. So much for that.

Using your training to teach others builds credibility, adds value, shows your colleagues and your clients that you care about your work, and that (although you may be inexperienced), you will do a great job. When people see that you have taken the time and effort to understand something so well that you can help anyone else understand, they will find you are worthy of respect, and referrals. Reinforcing and building your knowledge of real estate through teaching and sharing what you have learned can give you confidence while you are speaking with potential clients, and it will shine through to them. Therefore, your education in real estate is important, and sharing your knowledge with others is even better.

Enriching The Field For Others

Teaching other agents and clients is key to your own growth and to helping your clients feel more comfortable with you as an agent and a real estate expert. To take this to the next level, you need contribute to the industry in some way, big or small. By contribution to the industry, I mean that eventually you may find yourself writing a book to share your experiences with others. You might blog, submit articles for publication, podcast, etc. Perhaps you favor video more, and film Q&A's, how-to's. Maybe you value face to face interaction, and you can focus on teaching other agents. You can facilitate events, host networking events. Or contribute to real estate seminars. You might make some great closing gifts or other useful items. The time and effort is well worth it. By giving back, you get to develop your own ideas, and you get to share them with others in the industry.

To make this work, you need to focus on giving, and not expecting anything in return. People who create are valuable, and end up being well compensated for it. You shouldn't write a book or upload videos online expecting them to make you famous. You shouldn't offer something only for a financial or other benefit. You will do this to build your credibility, and to show anyone you interact with that you are an expert. The act of giving without expecting to get back shows that you can bring of value. Not to say that you can't or shouldnt start some kind of side business in the real estate industry, It may even do well. The focus of your giving back, though, needs to be on giving. Give value first, show that your training has paid off by helping other agents to do their job. The influential businessman Earl Nightingale once made an anecdote about this. He likened the attitude of wanting to get before giving to that of someone demanding heat from a stove BEFORE you gave it wood. You have to fuel your fire before it will give you heat. If you offer your knowledge and create value first, people will see that you know what you are talking about. That will enrich the industry's marketplace of ideas, develop your expertise, build a positive reputation, and make you a better agent.

Reputation

In order to be a successful agent, you need a good reputation. A reputation is the public's opinion of you as a real estate agent, and as as human being. If you are the best agent ever, but are socially unbearable, your reputation will suffer. If you are an awful agent, but have the most amazing people skills, your bank account will be wanting. There needs to be that balance between business skills and social skills. This balance between personality and salespersonship will help other agents, prospects, current, and past clients have a positive opinion of you. Positive opinions lead to positive remarks to friends and family. Positive remarks build a positive sentiment and a positive reputation. This doesn't happen with one transaction, it happens over many transactions. It can take a long time to build up momentum.

Even with the time it takes to build that reputation, it is well worth it. Striving to please your clients is a worthy goal. Having all kinds of well wishes, and nice words among past clients' friends and family turns directly into dollars in later years if you make sure to stay in touch. It is important to think about how you want your reputation to work for you over time. The best kinds of calls are when someone calls and says "Hi, I'm getting ready to sell my house, and my uncle said you were the best agent to call." Or "I don't know if you remember me, but a few years back you helped my friends find a house and I'm about to start looking too." By giving clients a great experience, you are building a reputation. Work on your reputation as a business building activity. Put thought and care into your client and prospect's experience. In the short term, you will have happy clients (which is what we all want). In the long run your reputation will precede you, then business will slowly and steadily flow to you.

For the new agent, the idea is to try to put yourself out into the real estate market and show people how well you can do. Eventually, when they are ready to buy or sell, your reputation will kick in and get you a phone call. Some agents I have worked with, who have been in the business many years, almost exclusively work off of referral and past client business thanks to a glowing reputation. They have been established in their community, and have done some great work there. So when anyone in their extended network is looking for an agent, they ask a friend or family member, and get referred to the one and only agent that comes to their minds.

No matter how well an agent is doing, few can afford to turn business away. Even those agents who are having great financial success rarely turn down more business unless they have to. No one in their right mind would send prospects and clients away from them. A bad reputation, however, will send clients running. Those should be very few and far between. The agent who doesn't take care to build a positive experience for each and every client, or the agent who doesn't care, will quickly build a bad reputation. It takes years to create a massive positive reputation. It will take about an hour to create a massive negative reputation. You can see this for yourself. People who feel wronged, or who are just angry, will go very far out of their way to share. An agent can not afford to lose business because they didn't take care of their clients, especially a new agent starting out. A series of bad reviews right at the start of their career can be very difficult (not impossible) to overcome.

No reputation at all is not as bad as a negative one. However, this can be a huge obstacle that many newer agents strike. This was a painful experience for me when I first started, and I did lose some opportunities because the client simply wanted someone with "more experience," of "someone who has more connections in the market." Whenever I am turned down, I focus on what that person said or thought at the time. I try to read between the lines and ask myself, "what could I have done differently that would have brought so much value to this prospect, that this issue wouldn't have existed?" Or, "what should I have not done..." Everyone makes mistakes in their presentations, they make mistakes working on a deal, they make mistakes with their clients. I haven't met one agent who was always perfect. If you want to build that positive reputation, keep making contacts and growing your business daily. Treat each lead and each client like gold. If you find that someone had a bad experience, try to remedy it. Take each negative as a learning opportunity.

Close the Deal

At the end of the day, the point of being a real estate agent is to close the deal. Ideally, you will be closing many deals a year. The best steps you need to take in that direction will be built on a strong foundation. Your foundation will depend on your skill set and services you render. You will be a real estate professional, conducting your business and behavior as such. You will be a productive member of your community. You will be collaborating with your fellow real estate agents, and helping your clients to live their lives (and get a good deal). You are constantly learning and developing your business skill and knowledge. You will use this hard earned knowledge and skill to give back to your real estate community in a way that can help other new agents and real estate professionals. You will, meanwhile, be building a positive reputation that will act as your own personal business magnet 24/7.

Those ideas will help you become a better agent, and build a successful business. Your successful business will be based on the ability to close a high enough volume of deals, over a short enough period of time, to not only help those clients and colleagues, but to also help yourself. The entire process from getting clients, negotiating offers, inspections, contingencies, attorneys, and all of those many layers of complexity are all designed for one purpose. The purpose is to take a real estate buyer and seller, and helping them agree to exchange $x, at x date. It's the close. A seller and buyer both agree to a date, and on that date they trade money for property. Close the deal.

Why Your First Year Is The Most Difficult

Least Profitable

If you are new to real estate, building momentum can be difficult. If you are new to sales, developing the necessary habits to consistently generate leads and follow up will take time. It is not unusual for a new agent to close only a handful of deals in those first 12 months. Some new agents are aware of this, and keep a second part time job, or keep their current full time job while they are learning the ropes. Their first year will be the least profitable.

If you want to make a living selling real estate, most of us will need more than two or three closes a year to support themselves and their families. Real estate agents are running their own service business'. Mounting bills, and other costs of living make up their business overhead. For many starting agents, the overhead can be higher than their net income. Money that I made in the first year didn't not cover all of my necessities, never mind the novelties. That environment brought on extreme stress, especially when I had no idea of what I was doing wrong. Not enough sales in a short enough period of time is a huge contributor to new agent's getting licensed, getting frustrated, and dropping out in a few months. Some folks literally can not sustain themselves and have to find another job. Cash flow is the single most important factor in any business. We all have to earn money just to survive, even more if we want to live.

There is hope, though. Although you are facing your least profitable year, there are things you can do to make it profitable enough. First, you need to tackle your budget. You need to figure out how much money you need to earn to survive. Then, how much does it cost for your family to enjoy their lives? You are going to set high goals, but you are also going to know the point where you can say you are safe, and rest easy. You can take your overhead and do some math. Say you need $70K to pay the bills, pay your taxes, retirement, food, clothing, vacation, and 52 nights-out with your significant other (or friends) for your first year. If you can take an average of 3% cash per deal at a 50%/50% split, than you need to close about $4.6M in total business that year. A 60%/40% split brings it to $3.8M. Meaning, depending on your split you need to close 15, or 12 deals averaging $300K respectively. That means you would want to close between 1.25 and one deal a month to reach your target. If you start on a graduated pay scale that grows with each close, or you can negotiate for a higher commission, it will be even less than 1 close a month. That means, that in 30 days you can focus all of your energy in closing one or two deals. Anything after that is icing on the cake. Maybe in order to live the life you want, you need to close 30 or 40 deals, but to cover your cost of living you need nine. Everyone's plan will be different, but everyone needs a plan.

Lack Of Expertise

Simply put, your lacking in expert skills or knowledge when you are first going in. Most new agents are learning on the fly, trying to make ends meet at the same time, which compounds a lot of stress and makes it more difficult to slow down and focus on mastering the trade. There is a lot of knowledge required for agents to successfully execute their duties. Some people can throw themselves into the fray, learn on the go without studying or working too hard, and make a good living. If you can do that, if you can break in to new and unfamiliar territory with any measure of success, bravo. You are also very rare indeed. We all know someone, or have seen or herd of someone who seems to be able to succeed without effort. Truth to be told is that most of them put a lot of effort into appearing effortless. The more experienced agents who just seem to be swimming in business without doing anything at all have been building a network for years. As you go, you will develop personal systems and schedules for your work, and you will streamline them for efficiency. Anyone can learn to implement systems, and those systems will make you so efficient that it will look to others that you are putting no effort in at all. Knowledge and expertise used to take action can give you very big results. The problem going in is that some new agents don't know the industry, and many others (myself included) knew almost nothing about real estate going in. Books like these, mentors, and other trainings will help you hone the necessary skills. We do not live in a world where encyclopedias of knowledge can be downloaded into our brains for immediate use (yet). We need to study, talk to experts, think, and we need to use that knowledge to help us take actions that bring us closer to our goals. There is no way around it. In order to be successful, you need to be an expert.

Experience

Like expertise, experience has to be earned over time. Experience is a word we use to talk about things we have done; in order to earn it, focus on things you will do. At first I lost some business because I was "inexperienced." A new agent must accept the fact that some buyers or sellers would be more comfortable with a more experienced agent. Take it in stride, and see if you can refer a colleague (or mentor) to step in. That way you can take a referral fee, and build a positive reputation in your office. Turn every loss into a win if you can, no matter how small. You are earning experience. Go out to meet people, and when it doesn't go as planned, take notes and review them. Talk to a colleague, read a book, use an audio program, anything. Turn every negative experience into a learning experience. If you are constantly taking action, and making the very most of your successes and failures, you can drastically steepen your learning curve. If you can stay with it, you will begin to realize success.

Another important point is to learn from others experiences. You don't need to touch a hot pan and burn your hand after you saw it happen to someone else. If you become aware of a fellow agent making a mistake, notate it so you don't make it as well. If one person struggles with lead generation over the phone, don't give up on it. The same goes for anything else. There is a difference between someone failing where they are unskilled and needs more practice, and bad business. Some things are obvious, and others fall in a gray area. You will be the judge whether to adapt a certain behavior or avoid it. It is important that you pay attention to others, and to see whats working, and whats not. Adapt others successes and avoid their failures wherever possible. Take into account their skill levels, and see if you need to train up on something before you give their technique a try.

Competition

There are probably agents with established brands and reputations working in your area. This means that you are going to have a hard time carving out your own space. Multiple agents competing for business in a certain area is a good thing though. It keeps commission rates under control (no monopolist is going around charging 15%, or 20%), and it forces them to be more pro active. This results in better client service. Competition forces people to work harder for less, meaning that the end user gets more service for less money.

However, while competition is good for buyers and sellers, it is very frustrating to lose business to a fellow agent. It's unfortunate, but it happens. You may get a difficult or unresponsive lead. You may meet with someone a few times who ends up deciding that they didn't want to move anymore.

Sometimes people will tell you that they "were only thinking about it," and that they can't go anywhere until after … whatever. Then, boom, they list their house with another agent in a few days. These prospects are either not serious about transacting anytime soon, or they want to be more polite than just telling you that they dont want to work with you. The latter scenario occurs of there is no perceived value in you or your services. The way to bring more value, and compete with more experienced agents is through training and hard work. If you are moving in to real estate to care for yourself and your family, you need to find a competitive edge wherever you can, anything less will result in unsustainable loss of business. Of course, when I say "loss of business" I am talking about the deal swept from underneath you by a competitor, and any leads not earned or contacted in the first place.

There are two types of competition you will need to confront: active and passive. Active competition is that buyer or listing snatched up by a competitor. Passive competition results when you fail to look for a buyer or seller or waited too long to respond to. Six months into my first year, I saw a FSBO sign in my neighbor's yard. I would see it, and the seller's phone number marked on it's top, every single day through the window. I didn't even have to leave my house, and there was a FSBO lead literally right in front of me. I let it slip through my fingers. One day I woke up to a for sale yard sign from a local agent! I was kicking myself when I saw that, and I had convinced myself that it would never sell, and when it expires I would be the agent to put it back on the market and save the day. It sold two months later. An agent went out and did her job. Sometimes new agents "can't catch a break," and look hopelessly on as other agents are swooping in and out and moving the market. You can never get business that you don't actively work for. Yes, sometimes people come to you, and that is nice, but you can't live off of the hope that enough people are going to reach out to you. Maybe one day will have a strong enough brand and reputation that you can cut back on marketing costs and sustain your business through an extensive referral network. For new agents, that is not an option for most of them. You will have to market yourself and actively generate leads in order to succeed.

Articulating Value

A value proposition is literally a promise of value to be delivered. In real estate, your value proposition is essentially what you do, and how you are going to do it. When you first meet with a lead, you are going to pitch yourself and your company. You are going to answer questions, advise the client, and explain to them why you and your company are the best suited to fulfill the client's needs. That may be obvious to some, but not many agents actually sit down and write up a value proposition. Gary Keller's book "The Millionaire real estate Agent" has a section covering this, and they offer a fairly comprehensive value proposition. If you have not read that book already, I would put it on the top of your "to-read" list for your continuing self-education. Without knowing exactly what you can and can't do, you are forced into using vague statements. A potential client wants an agent that is direct, knowledgeable, and can tell them what they are going to get. This does imply a certain degree of preparation. You need to learn about your company and what makes it unique. You need to think about yourself, and what personal touches you can add into the mix on top of normal job duties. Here' something I use to make myself stand out during a presentation:

"Some agents will list the house on MLS put a lock box on the door, then disappear. There are 'listing agents' and there are 'marketing agents.' I'm a marketing agent. I will take this property's information, all of my notes, and photos, then I will broadcast that information out into the largest buyers network in the state. Almost every buyer in the market right now is working with a buyers agent. I am going to make this information available to every buyers agent in the country with a client looking in this area and price range. I also leverage technology by developing targeted advertising, I will proactively put your listing in front of buyers who may be interested. We send out postcards, and use other marketing materials in your neighborhood to get people talking and develop interest. I saturate the market with your listing."

Scripting

Take notes on your presentations as they come along. Build a record of what worked, what didn't, common questions, and common answers. Write short Q/A style scripts to go over different scenarios, practice with a friend, or talk to yourself while driving in the car to practice. Know exactly what you do and what you offer, know what your company can offer, and by learning to articulate your value, you will strongly differentiate yourself from competing agents. This will help you practice standing out from the crowd, and you will be able to show clients that you are the best person for the job. Some agents may feel that to be a grand claim, and I'm sure there could be better agents out there. Remember that you don't need to be the greatest real estate agent on earth to get a client. You only need to be better than your immediate competition. You don't need to be miles ahead of them in business, you only need to seem a little bit better.

By fully and clearly articulating your value and your services, you will truly be the best agent to work with. Client's who understand and appreciate their agent are going to be much more satisfied.

Articulating value is important, and on the other end of the spectrum, a weak value proposition can hurt your chances. Saying things like, "we can help you sell your house" is fine. But what do you say when the response is, "OK, so what do you do that 'Super Agent X' can't do?" Some have more or less resources, more or less cash for tools, but the playing field is relatively level with a few exceptions. If you don't have a good answer to that question right now, what will you say? "Oh, nothing really, I was just hoping that you will work with me." That is a crucial moment, and that is when you need to sell yourself via your value proposition. It's true that most buyers or sellers go with one of the first few agents they interview. It is also true that there is nothing more satisfying than getting a listing with that client who does their homework and interview's multiple agents. Do you want to hope that they just sign on with you, and never interview another agent? Do you want to have certainty knowing that even if they interviewed 100 agents, they will still pick you? You want to get a call by those prospects saying "you raised the bar so high, the others couldn't compete," or "we don't know if its because we like you, but the others just couldn't hold a candle to you." and so on. Weak value proposition = giving the possibility of earning more business up to chance. Strong value proposition = signing contracts on the spot and more satisfied clients. There is a learning curve there, but extra time and preparation can turn that curve into a vertical line on the Knowledge-gained-over-time chart. Anything less is leaving your business, and your livelihood up to chance. Scripts can be found at your brokerage, or online if they don't have any to provide.

Small Or Untapped Network

A small or untapped network (your circle of influence) can doom your business. An agent can earn much repeat business from their personal network over the years. As you close transactions, those past clients also become members in your sphere or circle of influence. If every person you know has 100 friends and acquaintances, and they have 100 friends and acquaintances, accounting for overlaps, you could touch a huge demographic (thousands of people) through your network.

But what if you don't have a large network? Consistently marketing yourself to friends, family, and their friends/family can give you a few great deals over time. Some great ways of expanding your sphere is through networking. Social clubs and charitable organizations are a great resource. In a club or charity, you get to meet people, and integrate and establish yourself within your community (more later). I have met some agents that receive regular business, year after year, from groups and associations. There are networking groups specifically for business. There are seminars, classes, clubs, and your children's (if you have them) school and sport's events. Anywhere people congregate, you fill find someone who needs an agent, from obvious ones like landlord and realtor associations, to less obvious like special interest groups, horticulture clubs, and so on. Remember that every person you meet has their own network. You aren't just asking one person for business, you are positioning yourself to ask 100 people for business. There are more people who need agents than there are agents. Over 90% of real estate is being sold by less than 10% of the licensed agents. There is no shortage of business for those who are willing to go out and get it. If you increase the amount of time you have in front of others, you will grow your network, grow your business, and meet some fantastic people.

Another problem I encountered was that my network, while small, was also untapped. A network of even a large size that you aren't prospecting within, is worse than a small network. They do go hand in hand, but if you have a large untapped network, the steps are the same. The act of growing your network is a great opportunity to begin tapping it for business. "Tapping" the network is just asking for business. Everyone has their own way of asking so use your own words, and it's especially important to practice. Practice in front of people, practice in front of yourself, think about it, write about it. Do not sound forced or awkward. Do not make people uncomfortable. You are offering a service, and you are helping people live their lives. You do not need to feel guilty, and you shouldn't feel negatively at all about it. In real estate, your livelihood hinges on closing deals, you can only close deals after you acquire clients. If you feel awkward about talking to your cousin or a stranger about using a real estate agent, you need to iron that feeling right out. Awkwardness is a wrinkle in the shirt of your profession, practice is the iron. The iron only heats up with energy and repetition. If you want to get better, you need to dive in. Everyone has their own style to develop, but you do need to develop it. Even seasoned professionals still go to classes and seminars, they still read books and talk to mentors or other professionals, they role-play and they practice. Real estate is not just a sales job. People do not come to you (except as mentioned above), you need to meet them and ask for business.

Irrelevant Guidance

Relevant guidance is simply advice that applies to you and your market. the key takeaway is that it is for you and your market. There are experts that you will talk to who are full of exceptional advice. I have endeavored to make every interaction with a more experienced agent into a learning experience. Every agent that has been working for a number of years has some tremendous advice to share, and has seen the market ebb and flow. The biggest issue I have run into is when soliciting the advice from an agent in a different niche or market, or when taking council with an agent working off of a completely different business model. Each agent can have their own unique approach to their work and be successful. However, every agent cannot use another's techniques exactly. If the only difference between you and a top producer in your market was the sound of your voices, you won't be able to adopt the same approaches without adapting them. Your appearance, your syntax, your energy, and your methods are unique to you. This also means that unproductive ventures for one agent, could be productive for you. The trick here is adaptation, practice, and an open mind. In my first year, I figured that I had learned everything I needed to know, and proceeded to ruin myself financially. In desperation I then studied successful people and tried to copy their exact behavior. I didn't think too deeply on that until my second year, but why would the best practices of an agent who makes $900,000 a year, and has a full time staff be my best practices? Obviously there are awesome takeaways in work ethics, presentation styles, marketing strategies, etc. There isn't anything wrong with cherry picking advice; in fact that is the only way to succeed. In your first year, a lot of things are unclear. You may not even have a "style" or any go-to practices to earn you business and work with clients. That is OK. You can adopt practices of other agents who appear to be doing well, but you need to track your progress. Take notes, make a chart, or just remember. If you try something new, and it works for you over a long period of time (well into your second year) then you should make it a fixture. If you try something new and it fails, then don't repeat that error. Remember that it goes both ways. Occasionally I take advice against something that I initially thought was a good idea. When we develop our ideas, we inevitably come across what we think is a real game-changer, only to find out that it was a dud. Other agents can sometimes see this coming, and when you are given advice against something, evaluate it first, but always take it if it is sound. Some advice will seem great and just not work out, old-bad advice will become worthwhile in the future, and profitable practices now may not be worth it in a few years. We always need to be on the cutting edge, if only to constantly verify that we are doing our best. If someone gives you a tip, think about it. Think about how it has worked for the advisor, and how it can work for you. The absolute worst advice to take is something that has not been tried. If someone is telling you about how lucrative a FSBO lead generation business is, ask them how it has been going for them. If the answer is something along the lines of "well, I've never done it, but it seems like a good idea." Even if it is a good idea you need to go talk to someone with experience.

No Previous Experience in real estate

Lack of experience can be a huge obstacle in any profession. In fact, lack of experience is the only barrier to entry in some cases. If you used to be an agent, and wanted to renew your license, you may have some of the same anxieties as someone with no background. You know so much more, that you probably know the company you will go work for, and the people you will work with, and about your day to day operations as an agent. Someone with experience knows how to get back into the swing of things.

On the other hand, having no experience can be a problem. First, because you may feel pressured into inaction because of insecurity; and second, you might feel pressured to take the wrong actions because of your insecurity. Some of us may lean to the inaction or action side, but we all know that jumping in to something new that we have no knowledge of can be problematic. The only real solution is training, research, working with mentors, and grinding through it. It may be a hard pill to swallow, but most agents starting today will need two to three years of work experience before they can start making a name for themselves

There are other tasks and responsibilities to consider as a first-year agent. As an agent you are self-managed, marketing, negotiating, scheduling, using internet resources and computers, filling legal documents, and coordinating services between vendors. For self management, you are largely accountable for your entire schedule. If you are normally working fixed 9-5 hours, or are used to knowing exactly what you will be doing and where for weeks or months in advance, the freedom and power agents have over their schedule might be a shock. I know it was to me, and instead of blocking/ chinking time, or using any organizational structure to my work I constantly found myself with nothing to do for days and days, and then working furiously around the clock for days, and back to nothing. If I had regulated myself and worked a steady pace every day I could have done more with less time. Just as important as setting your work hours and chipping away at your tasks steadily and with purpose, you also need to be accountable and reliable for your schedule. Never show up late to an appointment or cancel beforehand. Predict your schedule as best you can, and if you can't or aren't sure, it is better to set "tentative" meetings subject to change than to constantly miss them. When people are talking about you behind your back (and they will), do you want them to say:

"Oh, Agent So&so is ok. He gets back to you eventually."

Or, do you want them to say:

"If Agent So&so said he said he would meet you there he's going to be there, you can set your watch by this guy. If he tells you he is going to do something, it's going to be done.

Importance of Marketing

Marketing may be something completely new to you, but if you make sure that you talk to people about it and do your research, you can make some sound marketing decisions. I failed on both those counts. I assumed that if I spent money (no matter where or on what), people would call. They didn't and the expense didn't pay off.

One of the key marketing tools you have at your disposal is on the internet. The internet is a massive Information source, and any successful agent should put the time in to learning as much about using those tools as possible. Not having a website or social media presence is a disadvantage. Test this out, go to Google and input my name. What comes up? Now enter your name. If you have fewer hits, it might be worthwhile to do something about it. Remember that when someone first hears about you they might look you up in the same way.

It is true that most people sign on with the first or second agent that they meet, but people on the fence, or who really want to do their research first, are guaranteed to Google you and look at your online profiles and pages. What do you want them to see?

Managing the transaction

Legal paperwork and lender coordination is likely new to everyone breaking into the field. The forms need to be filled out accurately and correctly, and signatures and dates need to be spot on. Legally binding documents are an essential formality that is apart of a centuries old legal system. People have been using written agreements and contracts since before we had ships that could cross an ocean, and we are still using them today for a reason. Do your ancestors proud, and double check your dates and initials! Vendors, like attorneys and loan officers, are as essential to the industry as the agents themselves, but they don't always talk, and sometimes they are extremely busy with other deals. This means that they cannot devote as much attention to the deal as you can, and as the agent, you are in a unique position. You need to double-check documentation, make sure things are being done on time, and constantly follow-up with everyone to get updates or pass information around. Generally things go smoothly, but the one small silly mistake that no one notices could cost valuable time and money by prolonging or losing a deal. As an agent, you are getting paid to manage all aspects of the deal, including doing the math on figures on the P&S contract, verifying that the deposit amounts add up to the right figure, and that all clauses are written up correctly, or haven't been forgotten. Its all a formality until the close, but if something goes wrong, or someone gets angry and starts looking for a loophole, you don't want to let anything slip through your fingers, even if it was not directly your responsibility. That can be a lot of work, and especially stressful. Not many people have had to deal with legal paperwork or vendor coordination, but be ready for it. We all know about those perfect deals, and its nice to imagine that money will just rain down on us because we want it to, but if there ever is a mistake you will regret not being on top of it when the closing is pushed out for weeks because something was lost or incorrect.

Most companies have various degrees of training to help you cover a lot of this in person, and in depth. Most importantly, if you approach it with an open mind and energy, you can get it done! The others working on the deal with you would be more than happy to help as well. Advice is free, and they get paid on the closing too, so you can count on them wanting everything to go through as well, and therefore wanting to help you facilitate a smooth transaction.

What You Need To Know Going In

Real Estate Is A Job

Being a real estate agent is a job. In order to be successful in real estate, you need to give it the time and attention it deserves. It is a job, and especially when you are starting out, you can put a full 40 hour work week in every week, and still have things to do. It's work, and sometimes it's a daily grind. You don't just show up when you feel like it and call a couple people to make a deal. If your expectation was that you could make a comfortable living working a few hours a week here and there you will be desperately disappointed. The key to success is to keep a constant flow of business, and that is tied to lead generation and making appointments. You found a buyer? Great, set an appointment, prepare for it, now get some more leads. You got a listing? Congrats, set a follow-up/ marketing plan, and get more leads. The work needs to be done every single day. My greatest failure in my first year was celebrating too soon, and not thinking about the future. If you are used to a steady income, you need to watch out. If you get 5 listings, and find 10 buyers to work with in one month, you still need to get more leads and make more appointments. There is no guarantee that those 15 clients will lead to closed business, and there is no guarantee that they will close anytime soon. Even if you do have 15 clients to work with, and you close them all right now, say you take in forty or fifty thousand in commission, then what? If you can budget your cash out for as long as possible, even longer than 12 months, you will be leaps and bounds ahead of many. At that point though, you need to continue to generate leads. You need people to know you and know your name. People need to see you and hear you, you need to have a presence. If you stop for anything, you will lose your momentum. Honestly, if you make enough commission in your first quarter to cover you for the rest of the year and you stop working, next year you have to start all over again.

The importance Of Lead Generation

The most important aspect of becoming a successful real estate agent is to continuously generate leads. Leads are the fuel for your business. Working on leads turns into appointments, and appointments turn into buyers or listing agreements. Agreements turn into sales, and sales equal money. You need them, and what most people don't realize going in is how difficult it is to follow that road all the way to closing.

If you get 100 strong leads, you can maybe make a few appointments, say 25. From those appointments you can get 15-20 agreements, and then maybe ten closes.. to follow my reasoning than the numbers. When I say strong leads, I mean that they are people who are planning on buying or selling this year, whether they work with you or someone else. If your leads are expired and cancelled listings, For Sale By Owner's (FSBO's), internet, mail, sign calls, walk-ins, word of mouth, whatever, they need to be serious and ready. My experience so far is that those serious leads are more difficult to come by than you might think. I have even had people approach me, and insist that they are ready to buy. Then we go on showing appointments, Research properties together online and then decide that they don't want to move after all Those three hundred serious leads are diluted with people interested in the idea of buying or selling, ready to meet with an agent to talk about it, and ultimately backing out. So depending on your lead generation methods, you need more than three hundred. You might need a 1,000. This seems like a daunting task, calling and compelling lists and setting up databases. You will likely need to set up a customer relationship management system (CRM) to give you alerts and automatically send out emails (hopefully your company will provide this). It is hard work to generate your own leads, and to manage them, contact them, set appointments, etc. This is only part of the work, and part of what makes working as an agent a "real job." But how do you even get those leads? There are many, many methods of lead generation. Some companies provide leads. Some companies have programs in place toggle out a handful of seller leads every month, and it's up to you to make appointments and get the listings. You could also get buyer leads from the company occasionally. The only problem with refferall leads is that you usually have to pay a referral fee for each of them that close. Referral fees are common, and a fair way to do business, but if you depend on them too much, it can be quite a large discount on your income. If you are using your local multiple listing service (MLS), you will have access to their records and can search expired and cancelled listings, and check those addresses in the public records for names. Just a little research can yield full names and addresses of people who you know want to sell their houses, and you can use that list to send them mailers. My company also provides a service where, for the cost of materials and postage, I can upload a custom list, or set an automatic radius mailing, and design my own post cards and flyers to be sent out. This is a cool little service, and is relatively cheap. I mostly use it for "just listed," and "just sold" cards to promote myself and my listings in the neighborhood. Some companies provide reverse lookup services where you enter a name and/or address and are given that person's contact information. There are even free databases online that can find phone numbers for you. It is not a guarantee for every single address, in fact they can be quite inaccurate, but it's not an awful place start. There are also online lead generation tools that are in my opinion overpriced, and produce weak leads. I only use online lead generation and ads in conjunction with mailers and phone calls so I can saturate a certain market, otherwise I have found it not to be cost-effective. There are services that also provide complete lists that you can buy, or for a monthly fee you can have "unlimited leads" and access to their database.

All these methods can boost your leads up to 1,000 or more. You can spend a lot or a little money doing it; it depends on how much effort you want to put into aggregating them. The important thing to remember is that you should not do this all at once. It should take some time for you to research the best methods for you, and even try a few different ones out (I recommend starting with the cheapest first). You can give yourself a few days, or even a few weeks to put your list together and organize it as you please. You can target expired listings or for FSBO's, or you can even target a demographic within that group. In fact, in your lead generation efforts you can begin to think about niche markets that you might want to target (more on that later). Ok, so lets say you have given yourself three weeks to research your lead sources, pick one or more, and toss a list together of as close to a thousand names, addresses, phone numbers, and emails. Great job, now what? Again, this depends on how you want to approach it. What works the best for me is to use multiple modes of marketing. I use a combination of email, phone calls and mailings. I recommend trying more than one, but not necessarily all at once. Most importantly, you cannot stop. However you do it, you need long term exposure. Think of all of the ads you ignore or junk mail you toss every day. Things only catch your eye when you are in the mood, and you are looking for something specific. Even then, how many mailers do you respond to, or marketing emails you actually open and read? Probably few to zero, and that is normal. It's a lot of work, but it needs to be consistent. Phone contacts, referrals, and personal visits will produce the greatest results. It is just more difficult to ignore someone in front of you or over the phone. Do understand though, some people are ready to be very rude to a stranger calling or visiting them. Even if you have five thousand numbers to call, and you have gone through hundreds and hundreds, one person can throw you off course. At first I used to take those kinds of responses personally, but I have since learned to take it in stride. Some days I will still find myself loosing energy, or just loosing stamina to make it through any more contacts for the day. In situations where you might feel the same, or even have trouble getting started, this is what you should do. Call someone who loves you! Your friend's, and family are all in your sphere of influence, they are all people you know. Even if you just saw them only minutes ago, give them a call. Reach out to someone who you know will make you feel better just by having a nice chat. Catch up with old friends, check in on your parents or spouse, just take a couple minutes to enjoy a guaranteed positive call. This will have you feeling much better, and should be the boost you need to keep going until you have reached your goal for the day.

As you power through your list you begin to realize how time consuming it is. There are a few things you can do. After you are making some cash, you can increase your overhead and use an auto dialing service. There are services that you can use to upload your thousand person list, and it will call one line at a time, or sometimes three lines at a time. If you reach a voicemail, it automatically plays a pre-recorded message, and if the person picks up, it connects you instantly. Those services can help you make literally hundreds of calls an hour, leaving voicemails and reaching people at the same time.

Otherwise, you will need to block off some time every day, and call down the list. I have found a comfortable routine in waking up early in the morning, enjoying my family with some breakfast, and then sequestering myself in my office for an hour or two and try to make around 20 calls. I do this Monday through Friday, and leave the weekends for family time and/or showings and open houses. I can call about four hundred people a month, but it is usually much less because when people actually pick we talk for a few minutes. My daily target is 20 and I can blast through list after list over time. This works best for me because I can set appointments, and build up some good momentum that lasts into the day. You can use a similar method, or maybe something completely different. It is most important that you create a system that works for you, and you chip away at it every day on a consistent schedule.

Leading With Income

When you are leading with income, you are literally letting the money coming in set the pace for your expenses. I remember seeing the movie "Field of Dreams" when I was but a young consumer. In the movie, a farmer hears a voice whispering "If you build it they will come." The "it" turned out to be a baseball diamond in his corn field, and the "they" were the ghosts of past baseball legends. When the farmer decided to build the field, the ghosts appeared and played a game. The farmer decided to destroy a whole lot of his crops to build the baseball field based on the idea that something would happen after it was done.

When I got started as an agent I had that field of dreams mentality. I thought that if I simply built the infrastructure for making deals happen, that people would just come up to me and dump money at my feet. Obviously that didn't happen. high-cost, low-return lead generation, and other tools and technology that would indeed be helpful to agents who already had a ton of business was a waste of money for me. Until you have a stronger book of business, and a marketing budget huge up-front investments should be deferred to another time. I made the mistake of leading with expenses, I created such a large overhead, that every dollar I did make was going towards expenses from weeks and months ago. I was building the field of dreams, sure that If I set up enough lead generation and other services, the leads would start pouring in. It never happened. I started getting business when I pushed for in person or phone contacts, not a field of dreams. Desperate for leads, I paid for an expensive Internet lead generating service that produced no dividends. Instead of setting some money aside for expenses, I paid for a service with money I did not have.

What I learned is you need to monitor your spending. Think of how you can spend the absolute minimum to do the best job you can. If you need professional photographers or staging, your minimum will be different from someone who can use photos from their phone's camera, etc. Everyone's budget is different, and how they plan on getting the job done can be different, but do not go out and spend even $1 you don't need to. Even one extra dollar is a superfluous expense that you will regret when you tally the numbers. If you can control your expenses, and lead with your income you will be much better off. As you grow your business, and grow your income, you can up the ante. If you can sustain your current quality of life, or improve it to satisfactory levels. Do not go out and buy a new house, cars, or even an investment property. Use that money to invest in your business gradually. Begin to add on a stronger marketing budget, research more expensive tools to help your productivity. If you can do exactly the same level of business into your next year, then with your small improvements you should be able to add on even more. Grow your business gradually. Then over time, when you have regular income coming in, and money in the bank to cover a bad stretch or emergencies, and invest as you please. Remember that investment will be different for different folks. Some of you will want to hire an assistant to help you double your business. Some want to buy investment property, or stocks. Maybe you want to get your brokers license and start your own real estate company. Those are all worthy investment, there are very few investments, even on lead generation that grant an instant return. You cannot risk creating an overhead for yourself before you have the money coming in, it is foolish and dangerous.

The Importance Of Budgeting

You need to understand your finances, and be able to budget. Personally, I find budgeting to be the least enjoyable task of all, and I have a feeling that I am not alone. I have met a few people (not all agents) that really put work into their personal or business budgeting. They have printed or electronic reports archived, they fill out a spreadsheet on Excel every day, the whole nine yards. If you are like me, and do not have degrees and certifications for finances and accounting, filling out sheets and filling reports for your own books may not seem reasonable. Although that may be the best way for you to exactly track your cashflow and make financial decisions, it's not for everyone. On the other hand, most people I know just wing it, living paycheck to paycheck.

"hmm… I got my commission Thursday, the check should have cleared by Friday night. So If I add that to the negative balance I had before, and subtract the cost of the pool table delivery..."

-Declined-

"whoops, lets use the credit card"

Because you get paid only when you close a transaction in real estate, it's imperative to establish a budget and stick with it. You are running a business, and you can't let it fall apart. It's not just a business, it is your life. Because I failed to monitor my expenses I learned the hard way.

What I do now is use a budgeting software that is reliable and inexpensive that links to your bank, credit cards and loan accounts. Once you tag transactions and sort information, the software becomes automated. Most programs are either free or cost very little. Budgeting takes some time but it is well worth it. You can find free how-to's online for setting up your personal chart of accounts, and how to debit and credit them properly. The biggest drawback is the time consumption, the biggest payoff is your ability to make custom reports, and you get a more personal connection with your cash. Without a solid understanding of your budget and cashflow, you can't really say that you know your present financial situation. Without that crucial knowledge, you will not be as effective at making good financial decisions, from even the smallest purchases.

Your Colleagues Are Resources

As a real estate agent, you are in business for yourself. Your success or failure will be driven largely by the actions you take. While work can be done anywhere (home, office, coffee shop), there are some advantages to spending time with your colleagues in the office. I am talking about outside sources from other agents or professionals that show how far they can go, or what they do differently. It is so easy to fall into a rhythm and sustain it over a long period of time. This can be good or bad, but if you knew that you did one thing differently, and it would bring your business to the next level, wouldn't you want to try it? When you are with the same people day in and day out, you tend to pick up certain things from them whether you want to or not. Its very easy and comfortable to fall in step wit everyone else, or to use common practices. At one point, taking a colleagues advice or getting a new idea from them will greatly help you out, but if you want to grow as an agent and make a name for yourself, you cant always stay in line. For example, my first broker explained to me the importance of personal contacts and referrals. We assembled a list of everyone I knew so that I could begin contacting and asking for business. This helped me to close over $1 million dollars in business within months of my licensing. That is also part of what stopped me cold in my tracks. My broker had been in business for a very long time, and had such an expansive personal network that all he ever needed was personal contacts and referrals, and every year his list grew. For me, I had a relatively small family, and had fallen out of touch with many past associations while I was in the military. I struggled to fill a page worth of contacts.It wasn't until I was wrapping up my first year that I really began to study up on other successful agents. I read book after book after book, and it helped. I read books by other agents, books by game theorists, by top salesmen (not only in real estate), and even motivational speakers.I read at home in my time off, and I had over a dozen audiobooks that I listened to in my car instead of music or radio. I not only learned how there are agents in the world that make a $1 million annually year, I learned how they got to that point. Learning from those people helped me to reinvigorate my efforts and improved my morale.

Finding a mentor is important. Even if your broker or mentor has not written one, they have a novel's worth of ideas and experience that you can tap into. Even if you do not have someone working specifically as your mentor, you can become a mentee by finding a person of experience, and picking his or her brain at every convenience. I will do that to this day. If I meet someone with more success (or experience), I will initiate a friendly conversation, and get them talking about their business and their successes. Most people enjoy talking about themselves, and I enjoy turning that into a learning experience. Whether they know it or not, they are taking me to school. Every new agent should keep in mind that there can be a great learning opportunity with every conversation they may have. You don't need to take every idea to heart, but use the experiences of others to help develop your own ideas about how to run your business.

Negotiation

I have touched on this previously but being a skilled negotiator is essential for real estate agents. In my case, I had little experience negotiating in a selling situation, but as a social worker for homeless veterans I unknowingly got some good practice in. I would constantly find myself in situations where I was in front of people who simply did not know the advantages or benefits of a certain service, or simply had an incorrect or ill informed opinion of them. A veteran who insisted that he would never go to the Veterans Administration hospital because of bad military experience was passing over the opportunity for free quality health care, and many other benefits. This experience was invaluable when I made the transition to real estate. It also put more money in my clients' pockets.

You too can build on existing negotiation skills that you never knew you had. All you need to do is think about situations where you can convince people to give you what you (or a client) wants. You have done it before, even when it comes down to picking the restaurant, or what movie to see. People have very complicated negotiations every day, and often with more conditions, contingencies, and nuances than a real estate deal. Think about it, how many arguments have you've had about arranging your evening schedule? Agreeing that you can only make the five o'clock movie if you finish shopping and aren't hungry in time to make it to the theater. If you are hungry than dinner first, and a later movie. If you are not finished shopping, than grab a snack and go home to work on chores for a later showing. How about choosing a restaurant? What show to watch next? Who takes out the dog, is it your turn or my turn? You see, All of these decisions are made with some kind of discussion leading ultimately to a resolution, we are all negotiators. We already understand how it works, but we need to apply it in a new context. Buying a home hinges on the transfer of title. The entire deal is to facilitate that. Person A owns 123 Main St at 11:59AM, everyone signs some paper, Person B owns it at 12. That's what your client wants, and they want you to coordinate everything around it as their real estate professional. Your negotiations reflect that goal. You are talking about the sale price, and what any offers may be contingent on. You are talking about deposits and inspections, move in/out dates. The building's location and condition factor in, but at the end what matters is that the seller can get as many dollars as possible for the home, and that the buyer can pay as little as possible as the home. Somewhere in between them is the market rate, and the agents make it happen.

Anyone can learn to apply those life skills to real estate. Negotiating relies heavily on strategy and logic, and if you read up on those, or even take some classes, you will be far better prepared than most others. If you have a listing and a buyer approaches you saying that it is "priced too high over the town's assessment, no other homes are selling in the area, so what's the lowest you can go for me?" What do you say? I respond with: "1) The town's assessment for tax purposes does not reflect the market rate. 2) The neighborhood is extremely desirable and 3) the list price is X, and we will discuss all offers after they are submitted. Do you need my fax or email?" I know that I won't be swayed by other interpretations of value outside of the one I had already made, and although a given neighborhood may not be perfect, a perceived negative can be reversed into a positive, and most importantly, I will never disclose "the lowest we can go," or "the most we can afford.". Once you begin to work in the field, you will be amazed at the kinds of details an agent or seller/buyer will disclose once they get talking. Sometimes I start my negotiations with a friendly conversation, and anyone not fully aware that they are in a selling situation could let important details slip. Negotiations begin the moment you first interact with the other agent.

Strategy

Strategy in real estate is important. We touched on its gravity with negotiations, but you can apply simple strategic principles everywhere you go. When it comes to real estate, there are rules, and there are strategies. The rules tell us how to play, the strategies tell us how to win. You can't decide to simply follow the rules and best practices of others alone and succeed. You need a strategy. Everyone has certain styles or preferences that play into this. It is essential to learn from the top producers in the market, but what works for one agent in a particular area, may not work so well for you. It is important to take this into account when comparing others' methods to your own. Certain agents may have larger budgets to cover a larger area with print and internet marketing. Some agents may have a background in media or radio, and find success in radio ads and getting into local news stories. Some agents may be experts on their computers, and can design beautiful websites that draw widespread attention.

You might meet an agent that is making $300,000 a year in commission, you are told all about how they only use internet leads, and internet leads are the way to go for everyone. You can go out and make an extra car payment every month for this service right away, but you should first dig a little deeper. How long was that agent in business? What about referral leads, and yard-sign leads? How much money are they paying out for how many leads? What is their conversion rate? These are all very important questions, and you need to think about all of these factors when planning your marketing strategies. Generally, online leads converted and closed are among the most expensive. If that agent is only using the internet, you will likely find that is has taken an enormous up-front expense. One that may well be worthy, but is likely out of reach for the beginner. You need to think strategically, and lead your efforts with the money coming in first. Not hope that spending a ton of money will earn you anymore. We all know the "takes money to make money" adage, but that applies more to people who are already millionaires and make smart investments, not new agents. Think about what you have, and think about how you can spend the absolute minimum amount of money to get the best possible result that you are looking for. This means personal contacts outreach, cheap or free online presence through blogging or a website, and sending out inexpensive mailers done by hand or a reliable service. We have gone over some lead generation methods that are of low or no cost, depending on how you go about it. You can take those techniques and push forward. You want to make a name for yourself to bring in more business, help you gain more experience, and become an all around better agent. Keep in mind that there is competition. You must consider what other agents are doing too. If you only have the same or similar tools, then you need to perfect your value proposition. If you have something that no one else does, bring it up, and show your clients how you can use whatever tactic or gadget to get them a better deal. Put a lot of care and effort into preparing your information. Learn about the client and their needs as much as possible beforehand. Learn about their neighborhoods. For seller leads, even read their deeds and look up the market history for their home as far back as your records will go. Walk into every meeting ready to answer every question they may have, and be able to bring up important questions that even the owner of that home was unaware of. Use the same approach for buyers. Learn everything you can about them and their targeted neighborhoods. Research school systems and colleges. Look at restaurant and store reviews online. Show your clients that you care about them getting the best home, and the best deal. When I'm working with a buyer or a seller, I'm not even thinking about money. I'm thinking about how I can do the best possible job for them. My strategy: over-promise, over-deliver, and outwork my competition. It took me more than a year to figure that out, but I've been doing ok since then. Your strategy may need to be different, but following a well developed plan of attack can bring you closer to your goals than anything else.

The Various Business Models

Different businesses use various models to pay their agents. First, lets develop our understanding of commissions. Most of us know that agents charge a certain percentage of the sale price. The listing agent charges commission which is paid to a buyers agent, and very rarely the buyer's agent will charge commission from their buyers directly. The listing agent charges x% of the sales price, and of that total, the buyer agent commission is paid. For simplicity's sake, say the listing agent charges 5%, and splits it evenly at 2.5% per side (buyer/seller agent). From that split is where the agent's commission comes. If you are a broker without franchise fees or additional splits, you take the full 2.5% before taxes.

If you are an agent working under a broker, you further split your commission with the company. There are different business models that offer different splits and varying levels of additional services. There are some with low splits around 50%,but a high level of services. There are others with higher splits over 70%, with much less to offer. My first broker ran a great company where every agent was on their own. My commission was 75%, with no other fees or splits. Meaning, if I closed a deal with my buyer, and I was given a check of 2.5% of the total sale price, I would get three quarters of that (1.875% of the sales price). My commission before taxes on a 300K home would be about $5,625. However, I was given no marketing, no website, no leads, I had a home office, and I was completely self driven and managed. There were no office meetings, no collaboration. As an experienced agent, you can pretty well predict your income, and may prefer and excel in this kind of model. As a novice, it is easy to flounder. Another company I had done business with used a fixed commission at 50%, but they provided a bookkeeper, leads, marketing materials, 24 hours office access and more, all free of charge. There are others who use a graduating commission scale, where your first deal is 50%/50%, then after a certain number of deals closed, 60%/40%, and so on. Some companies will graduate your commission up with your closed business, and back down again if you hit a dry spell (usually not a huge jump down at once). Some offices offer lots of services, some offer few to none. Just be aware that there are other ways of doing things, and there are benefits and drawbacks to each. Depending on how you like to conduct your business, you may prefer the high-split/high level of services deal, and make a very lucrative living at it too. For anyone still thinking about that broker taking all of the cake, remember that it's just not as simple as that. As a broker you assume much more liability for when something goes wrong. Although you may want to shop around, ultimately settle with one that suits your needs best, not the one where you think you can make the most money (although you can have both).

Other Jobs In Real Estate

Other professions can include real estate photography, yard sign planting and removing, administration/assistant duties for the agent or office (great way to get started before you get your license), social media/blogging/article writing/web design or other like services (and agents need them), property management, and more. It might be worthwhile for some people to find a job in an administrative position part time while they take their licensing course, and use it to provide some extra income during that crucial first year. Nothing could better prepare you than to work with an agent (or agents) and see what they do to generate business. If you are not an agent yet, you might be worried about the commitment and finding out that it was not worth the effort. I would tell you that a new experience is always worth the effort, but you might be in a place in life where trying something new and starting over just wouldn't be a good idea unless you knew it was worth it. Fine, go work part time at your local real estate office in one of the job's mentioned. Put yourself into the machine, and see how it all looks from the inside. This way you can make money in the real estate industry without going all in, while learning the ropes.

Differentiate Yourself

Use A Niche Market

Essential for helping you to stand out from the crowd, a niche market is a great way to differentiate yourself from other agents. Niche markets are everywhere, just look at the specialty stores in a mall. Not everyone shops for eyeglasses, swords, or candles, but enough do to create a specialty market and a specialty store. One of the best ways to carve out your place in the real estate world is to stake a claim in a niche market. You can cover everything, or brand yourself as the go-to agent for

_____ . Anyone thinking that "real estate is a niche market," may be on to something, but like all industries there are often niches within niches. Each market has its own nuances. For example, in real estate there is commercial, residential, rental, multifamily, new construction, antique/vintage homes, time shares, and luxury properties. Each niche has its own stratified layers as well. If you are a commercial specialist, you could focus all of your business on leasing, or buying/selling. For commercial properties you could specialize in industrial buildings, office buildings, or plazas and stores. For residential you can focus on short sales, foreclosures, and so on. Rental real estate agents can manage property for others, or focus on working for management companies. Multifamily or investment property agents can work with investors and help them to grow their portfolios. Agents working in new construction can build contractor/ developer relationships and be the sole agent for the development. Antique specialists focus on classic homes, and can even brush up on their history to share that house's story with curious buyers/sellers. Time share agents can work exclusively on selling people a week or two of time at a resort or condo in a beautiful vacation destination. Luxury real estate specialists focus on marketing and selling those million dollar homes.

I did not have a niche my first year. I didn't want to brand myself a certain way because I was worried that I might drive away the only business I may get. In reality, if you specialize in new construction, you have to learn the ins and outs of your market and who is buying. At the same time, you are learning to differentiate it from other markets, and in learning one you learn about the others. If you meet someone that likes your work, but doesn't have or isn't interested in new construction, you can still help them. As a specialist in a certain niche, you prove your value as an expert in that market. I'm certainly not recommending that a brand new agent pick one market and run with it before learning all you can about all markets, but after your exploratory period (however long or short it may be), don't be afraid of losing business like I was. Specializing will help you become the expert of your market, and although you may drive business to your colleagues, it is better to earn one deal in a market you feel passionate about than to lose one in a market you don't like.

Every agent wants to set themselves up for success, and later focusing your attention is a great way to start. The only issue there is that there are likely other agents trying do do the exact same thing. All agents want to be successful, and many of them will take the right steps to reach that goal. Many of them wont consciously target a niche, they will organically fall into one if they are not paying attention by virtue of repeat business and referrals from one demographic more than another. That means that there are likely some untapped markets in your area. For example, imagine you live in a city, and the residential market is 90% multifamily's and rentals. The commercial market so dominated by a couple of big firms that no one has really broken into it in years. As a new agent, you are seeing this and thinking "well, I guess I'll have to start on rentals." If that is your plan, and that is where you want to be, perfect. If you would rather work on sales, then you can dig deeper to find your niche. Just because there is an agent around every corner, it does not mean that every market is covered. What about luxury real estate? Big city's have million dollar condos and townhouses, where are those agents? Maybe the market is covered, but there are 15,000 agents in your city, and Lux homes are only covered by 60-70 all together. Those firms might need some help, and allow you to pick up their leads and branding, or you can squeeze yourself in through another company. Same goes for antique homes, or you could even target condos in a specific area. Cities are always growing, and developers/investors are always coming in from out of town or out of state. They need agents, and if you position yourself right, you can be the only one they work with. This requires a high level of forethought and preparation. Although accidents do happen, and some huge developer or million dollar buyer might stumble onto your stoop, but you cant count on it happening. Look at your market and find your niche. Put yourself in a position to get noticed by buyers and sellers in your niche. There are high cost/high profile techniques, and its converse. If you cant afford national advertisements in developer's periodicals and long lists of leads, you probably can afford to join a few clubs and participate in your community. On top of that, everyone can afford to go out and meet people, even knock on doors. The nice is important because other agents on the outside will not receive the same opportunities. You become part of an exclusive group, where clients only want to work with the specialists, and actively look for them. If you want to sell new condos out of a new building, you need to make yourself a new-condo-construction-specialist, and make so much noise in that market that business comes to you, and when you go looking for business, that developer can look you up and see from your records that you know what you are doing.

Unique Pitch

What you have to tell prospective clients is as important as what you do for them. Practicing your pitch is the best way to get that message across.Nothing beats a great first impression, and you want yours to be so good that the only agent your prospects are thinking about is you. You want to master your elevator speech as well as your listing or buyer's presentation pitch. An elevator pitch is a short 20-30 second proposition. If you were taking an elevator and someone stepped in next to you, and that person had to get off on the next floor but told you that he/she needs an agent, your elevator speech will be compelling enough that the person will want to work with you. Your presentation will be somewhat longer. You may even find yourself in front of a prospect who is ready to make a decision within only a few minutes.You should develop your pitch over time, and use a value proposition. Get feedback on your pitch, alter it, and practice the updated version. You are doing this because you want to have a seamless and natural conversation where you can flood your prospects' mind with all of the great work you can do. Your pitch doesn't need to be comprehensive, however. I have worked with some people from initial phone call to close and they never learn about some of the tools and services I can provide. I always adjust my pitch and pay attention to subsequent conversations with the client. I don't need to explain my marketing plan to everyone in order to use it for everyone. Generally the home buying and selling process is the greatest expense people will make, and sometimes it's a very emotional time. Clients want to work with somebody who they like and someone who is competent. Since they will probably like every agent they meet, then they will stack them up against each other. Your pitch is a short conversation to show that you're more than just competent, and that you are friendly and likable. You are going to show them, or directly tell them depending on your style, that you care about them and you care about your work.

They need to know that you are not just there to collect a paycheck and forget about them. Time and thought put into a pitch accounts for this, and a great one will serve you well. Remember that you are selling a service, and you are selling you. That service costs money, and clients need to be comfortable with you, and they need to see that you are a professional who will get this job done.

There are many ways you can craft your pitch, and many free resources to help you do it. When I make mine, I keep a simple formula in my mind and write it down. I think: Why am I a real estate agent? What can I do that someone else can't do? What can my company do that others can't do? I write those answers and then every few months I do it again to see if I can improve it. You can use my method, someone else's, or develop your own, just don't neglect your pitch. It doesn't need to be especially long as well. In a selling situation, the highest form of persuasion is through asking questions and listening to your prospects. Use your pitch to establish yourself as the expert, then get right into your scripts.

Your Story

We don't normally think of our past in a linear fashion, and most of us feel that it isn't important. In fact, our story is very important, especially when meeting a prospect for the first time. There will be certain occasions that won't be ideal to share your story, but you can certainly add it to your presentation, or save it for the right moment. You can give your presence more context and more meaning to your clients with your story. Often enough you will find yourself in front of a stranger. This person has never seen you, and likely never herd of you before. If you can show them that you are a human being and a great agent, you will be more interesting and relatable. I used to hide my story. I was worried that I would alienate business and referrals from people who would not be able relate to me, and I didn't think I had that much going for my story in the first place.

Coming into my second year I began to really study successful people. I was absorbing all of this information in their videos and books, and anything else I could get my hands on. Then as I was learning about their stories, I realized something amazing. All of the high-performing professionals have a clear and interesting story. It answers an important, but unasked question. Why are you in real estate, and why are you here today? The story isn't a bland list of your previous accomplishments. Think objectively about your past, and every event that has influenced and inspired you to take those actions that led you to your present point in life. What consistent passion or behavior took you into real estate? What professions or studies helped you develop your interest in helping people find new homes? When I tell my story, I speak of military experience, and fascination with experiencing how people live in different cultures in Europe and the Middle East. I tell them of my experiences working for the state in support of homeless veterans after my service, which ultimately led to my career in real estate. I talk about my mission to help my clients live the best lives they can. I share my revelation that people in general are far more alike than they are different, no matter where on earth they are. In developing my story, I answered simple questions: Why am I a real estate agent? What am I passionate about? What experiences have I had that helped develop my passion for real estate and making sales? Anyone can ask themselves questions about their own past experiences to do this, profound or mundane. People remember stories and emotions much better than plain facts and dry presentations. Nothing leaves a good impression like a well-delivered, meaningful story. You may also notice something about yourself that you haven't before when thinking in this way. Developing a new kind of self awareness and self analysis will be an incredibly profitable business development activity, but it has implications in other areas of your life as well.

Services

The services you offer may be similar to competitors, but in order to make yourself stand out from others, you can present them differently. You can also do some extra research on your company's services, and see what extras you can add in, or alter in some way. When you are meeting a buyer or seller for the first time, you want to offer your services in a way that shows them how well you know your job, and how no one else can quite do what you do. You may want to develop those ideas and offerings into scripts or even presentation pages/slides and make your point explicitly.

Some services by their very nature stand out. You can offer professional photography and staging, you can offer "exclusive access" to a group of professionals that you know and trust for moving, financing, interior design, etc. You can offer highly specialized knowledge and demonstrate your expertise on the nuances of your niche, and use that knowledge to make predictions. You are going to sell a house, but what you are offering will help you execute the transaction and provide all of the other ancillary services to make it happen as smoothly and quickly as possible. In your presentations, you can even research into the best practices and other offers from your competitors and address them in your meeting. You can say, "with company ABC, you will get 'enhanced' online listings that bring your listing to the top of the results, but with my company you get that and a dedicated team of internet lead specialists who are trained to properly follow up and convert those leads, increasing our sales by x%, and helping us to decrease our listing's days on the market by an average of x. This means that we can market your property better, and bring qualified buyers faster and in greater quantities than leading competitors." Don't worry if that does not apply to you directly, the idea here is to find something that you already do that other agents are not doing. If you can pinpoint those special offers that you can do better than anyone, or that no one else is doing, it doesn't matter if you have been in the field for one year or twenty. At the end of the day, prospects choose the agent that they are most comfortable with, and who they feel is best suited for the job.

Tools

Running your own business requires that you have the necessary tools to get the job done. Many of these tools are free or cheap and a new agent take advantage of them. When evaluating any purchase, new agents must remember to spend the absolute least amount of money possible for the best result's. This means, only buy one lockbox (if they are not provided to you) for a new listing, don't buy 3 or 4 in anticipation of business, or because you got a package deal. Do not buy expensive folders and presentation packets, don't spend your commissions on expensive gifts (but you should gift), and don't go out and buy a brand new iPad, bag, cases, and $50 pens before you make any money. Add on to your gadgets and equipment only as you have a need. You certainly should treat yourself, but only with money you made, and within a reasonable budget. So your tools in the beginning are going to be mostly free. You probably have the implements of writing already, and even a laptop and/or tablet. You might even have a printer at home, or free printing available at your office. Use the tools you have and the ones given to you.

Physical tools that I use are a smartphone, notebook, pen, laptop, printer, and a binder for extra papers. Intangible tools I use are emails, postcard printing and mailing services, contact management services, online note taking applications, electronic document filling and signing applications. You can track and manage contacts in a spreadsheet or a similar program as for free as a beginner CRM, you can use free applications to fill out and sign paperwork (or just use paper for now). Your tools are only as effective as you are. Your chief concern should be on becoming a great agent, dont fool yourself with the "but if I buy this new tool I'll work even harder" excuse. Convincing yourself that the key to your success will be found in the next gadget is incorrect. The key to your success lies within yourself and your actions. The daily habits that you nurture and develop will build your business. The tools that people say help agents gat more leads and close more sales, only work when you already have the behavior in place, and the leads that come with it already. New agents developing their skills need to learn how to be effective before they implement complicated tools and processes that can be difficult to manage. Everything you could buy or add to your arsenal only supplements you, not your business.

Depending on your business model, or how your company wants you to operate, you will need to start off with some expenses. Some companies require you to join your local realtor association. There are also MLS fees. Other companies may offer to cover certain expenses, or not require as much. Some may even demand more, like following certain dress codes, desk fees, or certain technology fees that you must pay for. Your ancillary tools will vary, but the necessary core skills are all the same. Spend as little as possible on fluff, and stick to what you need.

Preparation

When it comes to working with clients, I adopt the Boy Scout motto: Be prepared. Being over prepared is the way to go; going into a meeting underprepared is not an option. If I am working on a $100K deal or a $1m deal, I am always ready. I do this to show that I am an expert, a professional, and that I genuinely care about what I am doing. You should prepare as much as possible for your first client meetings, and for all Subsequent get-togethers. Try to be passionate and professional so that your clients cannot help but to be excited to work with you. That excitement will spill over to their friends and family when they talk about you, and it could also help you earn more business. You know that you are not going to trip over a pile of money in the street. You know that you need to earn your living by doing the best job that you can, and even better than your competition. That's why preparation is so important.

There are some things that can only be mastered with constant repetition. Things like comparative market analyses are somewhat speculative in nature since all real estate is unique, and good comparative reports require a certain level of experience with your market. Having scripts and notes available to use is something I recommend for first-time agents. Some competing agents will prepare more, and some will prepare less. Some seasoned pros have incorporated systems to streamline and speed up the preparation process, but that does not mean that they are less prepared than you. The same thing applies to you. If you spend several hours preparing for a presentation, if you are putting materials together inefficiently and haphazardly, you are not more prepared than someone that knows what they are doing, and can do it in less time. Putting a presentation together will take you longer at first.

If you do not have materials ready to go, use your own templates, and have quick and accurate ways to run reports, you will need time to set it all up. I have seen listing agents who bring full 75 page reports with them to listing presentations that last in excess of two hours. Those agents almost never miss a listing opportunity, but it takes them an insignificant amount of time to bring everything together for it. They have been working for a long time, and know exactly how to generate an accurate customized report. New agents can borrow techniques from the real estate veterans who may share with them, but no two systems are identical for a reason. You will want to customize it to you so you can be as comfortable as possible.

I was not very prepared my first year. I saw top producers effortlessly tossing an information salad in seconds, an running right out to make their appointments. It seemed like they were not prepared at all. I thought "I can definitely do that. " I would go in cold, with basically no information. What I was seeing, but misinterpreting, was an agent who had a well established system for preparing for appointments. They had reports and other presentation materials already prepared or templated so they can plug in relevant data to customize it. They had internalized their scripts and their presentations to the point that it didn't take much effort to recall what they needed. They had so much industry experience already, that time spent studying wasn't as necessary. When I changed my thinking, and began to take myself and my profession seriously, I realized that was happening and I put the time in to create those systems. Wherever you see agents doing well with little or no work, what you aren't seeing are the hours, and often years of practice and real world experience that has helped them get to where they are. The good news is that you too can reach that level.

That first year will require time and energy. You are going to be investing a lot of time in preparing yourself. This may include research and asking for help or tips from a colleague. It may mean that you need to read more books, and spend more time thinking, planning, and executing on new or modified ideas. Practice scripts, role play, take note of your weaknesses and work on them. It is essential that you put as much time in as possible, and that you are ready to perform to the highest standards. No professional was born with the ability to present their services and sell themselves; it is learned over time.

Local Expert

Much the same as specializing in a niche, you can differentiate yourself from others as a local expert. You can target your home neighborhood, or some other geographic area that you know well. This has a few benefits. You may be the only agent who lives in that neighborhood. You are going to be better able to market yourself to buyers and sellers alike since you know the area better than anyone else, and know what it has to offer. You also have the benefit of low or no commuting time, which makes you much easier to get ahold of, and to hold accountable. Some people might not like the idea of living near their agent if they had a bad experience, but when you do a good job, they are going to appreciate it. This can be a mini-farm of yours, and can provide a lifetime of repeat business.

My first year as an agent I targeted an area that was 30 minutes from where I lived. That could work for some, but without an office there, or any other resources or experience, I was lost. If my office was in my targeted area, and I could go there every day, it would have been different. I only had a home office, and was constantly driving back and forth for meaningless little trips. Eventually I just stayed home unless I had an appointment. Of course, because I was not generating any new appointments with any vigor, I had days in a row of boredom, and then when something came up I would scramble around for a while until I found myself without anything more to do for another long stretch. I now have an office that I go to every day. If I don't have appointments I stay in the office, and if I have a lot to do that day, I might only pop in to print something, or sometimes not at all. I know my neighborhood. I live in it, and I work in it now. I am there nearly every day, and I know more about it than anyone visiting from the outside. I am a more valuable agent to anyone doing business in my neighborhood and community than I was as a transient in some other area, or a newcomer in mine. It has helped me to bring more attention closer to home, and saved me many tanks of gas. My first year was spent on the road, out of my community, and with no business.

Goals

You need them, and you probably have some right now. Perhaps reading this book is a part of one of your goals, or maybe you have been making some new ones as you are reading. If you haven't already, make goal #1 "Don't be like Tom Vargeletis when he started out." Now you are instantly better off than I was. The more you study successful people, and learn about best practices, the more you will learn about the value of setting goals. Every self-improvement, business, and basically all instructional material involve goals and goal-setting on some level. Simply, there are things you want to do, and it helps to keep that in mind over time. If you want to be a real estate agent, you need to have an idea of what you want to do, how much money you think you should make, and how you want your daily activities to look. Those are goals. I want to make $100,000 a year (goal), I want to sell houses (goal), I want to work less and spend more time with my family (goal). Things that we think about every day in terms of want or desire denote a goal. If you have something and want to keep or improve it, or if you want to have something in the future, that thought is a goal. Since goals are ideas that we hold onto and work towards, they affect our actions and the future. You are thinking of becoming a real estate agent, or have just started and want to learn more (goal), so you bought this book to help you (action). Goals lead to actions in order for us to realize them. Goals lead to actions, and actions generate results. If your goal is to become an agent, you will take action by inquiring about licensing courses, signing up, and studying. Sometimes your goal is to improve yourself in real estate, or gain more knowledge of your industry; therefore you take action by purchasing books, performing research, and talking to other agents about what has been working for them.

It is important to set lofty goals. This is because the scope of your goals determines the scope of your ultimate success. If your goal is to sell one house, you are going to take actions to realize that goal. If your goal is to sell 300 houses, your actions will follow accordingly. The key with goal setting is action. You want to take actions, and you will use goals to "keep your eyes on the prize" as it were, so you can stay motivated and push though the inevitable obstacles to realize your goals. The only thing that guarantees acquisition is consistent, relentless action. If we give up, change directions, or even lower our target, we are basically starting over and lose all momentum. A mediocre goal will lead to mediocre actions, and earn mediocre results. That is assuming that nothing goes wrong and we know that there is always something that stands in our way at some point. If you set an awesome goal, you are going to take awesome actions, and are going to have results that will inspire awe in yourself and those around you. As a new agent, my goal was to make as much money as I had the previous year, and to work less. My goal was so mediocre, and led to such mediocre actions, I had even less than mediocre results.

However, I did reach one goal. I worked a whole lot less than the year before.

Long Term Plan

Planning goes hand in hand with goal setting. You set a goal, you make a plan, then you take action. Plans are the maps for your actions. You can have special contingencies, multiple timelines, plans for both best and worst-case scenarios, you can make it as simple or as complicated as you like. Your plan is the table of contents to your story. Where do you want your story to go, and how will it get there? Once you have your goal, (say making $250,000 year; becoming a top producer in your market; impressing your family; anything, just aim high) you need to make a plan to accomplish your goal. You can make a short or a long term plan only, you can use both, or you can use a series of short term plans with mini goals in between (or milestones). It does not matter how you do it as long as you can stay focused and continue taking action towards reaching your goals.

I like to make general long term plans, and then put them into context with more specific and thoughtful short term plans, each with a goal at the finish line. I do this because it is easier for me to plan out my actions in the short term, with room to adjust if things don't go exactly as anticipated. Let's say that my goal is to close on one deal a day for an entire year, or 365 total closes. There is no way that I can possibly imagine that one person alone could handle that much business, so I will need help. I know that I will need an administrator and buyers' specialists, and even a listing specialist to work with me on lead generation and acquiring listings. Goal: 365 closings; Long Term Plan: Hire a few professionals to ramp up my lead generation to obtain more contracts. So what is my timeline? If my big goal is a finish line, then 365 completed closes is falling on Dec. 31 of a year in the future. If I want to close one deal a day, then I need to start on Jan. 1 of that same year. This means that I need to have my infrastructure and employees in place prior to this. I know that it is going to take time to find great hires, and to streamline systems in order to handle that kind of volume. Say it will take two years to hire everyone and build the systems necessary to handle this. Now my big goal sits at the end of a year, and it could take two years to work up to that point. So working backwards, what would it take to close 365 deals in one calendar year? Let's say that I'm a new agent, and I know I won' be able to hire anyone for the first year or more because I won't be able to afford the expenses while I still have debts and other living costs. This means that I have just developed an eight to 10 year, long term plan. I have milestones, and actionable steps leading up to my 365th close of my goal reaching year. Although that will be a long time from now, I know that about halfway there If I'm producing the right volume on schedule, I'll be making in excess of $200,000 per year, which I know can provide my family the life that we all want and deserve. In fact, half of that can cover my needs, including vacations and other enjoyable activities. Pick a big goal, and work backwards like this. Think realistically, and use this kind of thinking to create a plan that will help you take consistent action. Even if you fall short of the

goal, would you rather fall short of 10 closings a
year, or 365?

Short Term Plan

The short term plan comes next. Playing off of the reasoning of my long term plan, I can spell out the rest of my current year, and the next two afterwards. Your plan may be different, but your reasoning should follow similar lines. Now that I know in fairly general terms how I can reach my 365th closing in one year, what am I doing right now? I need to increase my production in order to be in a financial situation where I can seriously begin posting the job and taking applications. If I want a full time administrator, then I'll need to pay this person. Say the going rates for admin' are between $30-50k a year, depending on your location and the admin's responsibilities. If I can make an average of 3% per transaction, I need to close $1-1.7 million in sales volume to cover salary alone. There will be additional expenses, and as a personal touch I would add performance bonuses as incentives to keep motivation and production high. Realistically I will need to close $1.5-2 million alone to cover one salaried employee. I want to make a minimum of $200,000 in commission for that year, and my employee salaries and cost of sales can come out of it. This puts my volume at $6-7m for the year at a 3% average commission. I personally know agents who have closed volumes in significant excess of that number without help. It is not just possible, but even smaller brokerages have agents performing at this level. You may hit this point and decide that life is good as it is, and you dont want to work any harder. Beware of the "good enough" bug. You may hit $80 or $90k in commission and live the life of your dreams. That is great, and no one will look down on you for having 'enough' and staying there. The only problem is: once you have reached your peak, the only direction left to go is down. When you are at the top of the mountain, the very next steps you take will bring you down. Letting go of your dreams and settling down with the "good enough" bug, you are going to loose the momentum that brought you there. If you want to set a lofty goal as I recommend, you need to keep pushing until you reach it. Even change your goal as you approach your original target. Once I reach the year where I am closing over 300 sales, I'll just change my goals to close two a day instead of one. I recommend to always adjust higher, not lower.

Let's make closing $6.5m our minimum target for our short term goal. At that point we can hire people and move into the next phase of our business. That is because with each hire, you should see a 30%-50% increase in your volume. Some top producers double their last year's volume with their first hire. Either way, no matter how you look at it the first hire moves into the next leg of the long term plan, and getting to that point is a feat unto itself. If my average sale price is $250,000, the number of sales to reach $6.5m total volume will be on the order of 26 deals for the year. Let's round up to 30 for good measure, and make a goal to close 2.5 sales a month.

The top producers in the real estate business are the ones who focus on listing properties. You can have 20 listings, run open houses, work with buyer agents, take appointments all without risking insanity. If you had 20 actively looking buyers, you would be in a whirlwind of activity that will quickly drain you of any energy and ambition you may have. Another good thing about listings is that you get to put your name on a sign that people see and you can market yourself and your personal brand along with the home.Listings are also a great source of buyers. They may not buy that house, but they may buy another one with you as their agent. Many buyers have their own homes to sell as well. One good listing can indeed lead to three or more great opportunities to close sales. If you can find listings to find on your own, you can also work as the buyers agent for your sellers who need to purchase as well, and as a buyers agent for any unrepresented buyers who contact you about one of your listings. If you prospect and convert only 15 listings, or 1.25 in a month (one a month plus an extra four throughout the year), you will be able to build momentum in your sales business by all of the additional leads you can generate with them. Now the numbers are not just looking reasonable, they are obtainable, and that first hire is practically within our grasp. If you really push for the business, you can crank out much more than this. In the first two months of my second year I took six listings, and still had a mountain of leads to sort through. Other agents did more, but most agents do much less. This all hinges on your ability to hold your goals in your mind, and do everything that you can within your power to reach them. This does mean that you're going to have to work. Just remember that a little dedicated time and discipline now, turns into riches and happiness later.

Setting Milestones & Reaching Them

Creating milestones or mini goals along the way are important in helping you reach your long-term goal. Your big goal, 365 in 365, is what keeps you going in the long run. But what am I working on today? My long-term plan maps out how I am going to get there in general. My short-term plan helps me know what I need to begin working on this year and next year. For every plan, there are milestones: numbers of closings per month, number of listings taken a month, average sale price, etc. Start by focusing on the short-term plan. I need to have a sales volume of $6.5m at the close of the year. So it should be fair to say that once we are 50% there, we should have 50% of our target production. This means $3.25m volume in 6 months. That's a commission of $97,000, not bad for a few months work. It is possible, it's about 13 deals averaging at $250,000 if I can take an average of 3% commission. If you can take a minimum of 2 listings per month, and work with one buyer per month, the odds of you closing 13 deals or more tin time is very high. It's that simple: One listing a month, one buyer a month, 2 close's a month. Now, your day to day is going to reflect those goals. Odds are that most serious sellers or buyers will go with the first or second agent they meet who brings them value. Even if you decide not to follow my earlier advice on mastering your presentation, if you make up to two appointments per day, five days a week, you should definitely take one buyer and one listing in a month. So your next marker is to have met one or two people in a day. If this does not happen, you are behind schedule. If you are behind schedule, do not lower your targets to meet your current production, just pick up your pace, or maximize productivity in eliminating inefficiencies. At the same time, you need to generate leads. Your daily milestones should always include some form of lead generation each day. Some daily goals that you might have could look like:

1: wake up by 5 a.m.

2: write for 1-2 hours, eat breakfast, then prepare for day

3: lead generation, acquire one to two appointments, or follow up with past leads to work on setting up appointments

4: attend appointments

5: review and update notes, plan out tomorrow, make final prospecting calls or notes on priority tasks for the next day.

That's it, five daily goals, you can have more or less if you like, depending on how productive you want to be. Try to set daily, weekly, and monthly goals in this fashion. Do not write out a list once and plan on following it every day exactly, with no exceptions either. Do this exercise regularly, it would be best to do it daily. That way you can add, or even develop your goal ideas from something simple like 'generate leads,' to 'make 150 contacts, and a minimum of two appointments before lunch.' This flexibility will keep your mental gears turning, and allow you to stay laser focused on the important day-to-day activity. Take 5 minutes to write out your goals in the present tense, as if you already have them. Throw in a few for the next day as well. Over time, you will find that you can accomplish most of those goals that you consistently focus your attention on, and this exercise will keep them on the top of your mind for the long term until they are complete.

What To Do When Behind

When you get behind on your goals, it can be tempting be content with what you have accomplished. I do think it is important to appreciate your current successes. I'm not going to tell anyone to ignore the great things that they have done. I will tell people not to celebrate too much, too early, and I will remind them (like I have to remind myself) that every step in your journey needs to take you closer to completing a goal. If you find yourself at a point where it just seems like you are making no progress, keep pushing. Never reduce your target in order to make yourself feel better. Lowering the bar to make myself feel better was a habit from my first year as an agent. I didn't just lower the bar, I threw it on the ground. I was patting myself on the back for doing nothing. So long as I was convinced that I was doing enough by lowering my standards, I was enjoying a very fake and short-lived happiness. As a new agent, you will have the opportunity to set high standards from the get-go, and build successful habits right away. If you can aim high from the beginning and sustain your goals and activity over the long run, you won't fail to reach success. If you have small goals, or even none, you are going to take ineffective or zero actions, and you will be building a habit of mediocrity.

When you are behind, you need to catch up. You don't make a plan just to feel good about yourself and forget about it right afterwards. You make plans to provide yourself a map to your future, and your map is of actions, not getting excited for a few hours and then pretending that making a plan is all you need to do. You need to set your goals and milestones, and you need to take the necessary actions to reach them. You need to work hard and push forward, whether it is easy or whether it is hard. Sometimes we all get behind. We get sick, emergencies happen, or the work is just more difficult than expected. That is all normal. Everyone gets behind, but everyone does not put in the extra time to catch up. What can help you significantly is note taking, and tracking your progress. If you are constantly learning about what works the best for you, you will be able to take those best practices and ramp them up for a short period of time. You can push yourself and make double appointments for a couple weeks, or double your lead generation time. It is easier to increase activity and reach your targets than to lower your standards and trick yourself into feeling content about not performing.

Budgeting Money And Time For Work

Let's assume that right now, you already have your plan. You have a goal, or goals. You have a roadmap of your success in terms of long-term and short-term plans, with identifiable milestones and simple actionable steps. Part of that equation is getting started and building momentum, but the rest of your life needs to be spoken for as well. You may have a family that depends on you right now, or you could be flying solo. Whether you have no responsibilities, or even an ill family member that needs constant attention, there is always a way to find a work/life balance. It may be impossible to balance the two out evenly. Some people may be able to accomplish perfect balance in one form or another, but it rarely lasts forever. In fact, we all ideally want to have an unbalanced life skewed to our personal time. Many of us would be happy without any balance at all if only a small portion of our time and energy were spent at work, with the rest on vacation. Some people may not be able to imagine a life without constant work, and their happiness may be found in the same kind of unbalance.

The point I am making here is that a fully equivalent balance with your work engagements and your personal engagements is unlikely, and in most cases unwanted. We all live in unbalanced times, and throughout life things can happen that forces us to re-adjust, or re-prioritize earlier commitments. Many newer agents already have set routines, or families to care for, kids to spend time with, you name it. We all have different abilities and different responsibilities. You are physically able to work for 10 or 12 hours every day, but "loved ones" will no longer be so if you keep that up for too long. If your work/life needs to be skewed toward other important aspects of your life, than embrace it. You can succeed with less time on the clock, you will just need a work around. Your physical time constraints can help you to develop systems or more efficient methods for accomplishing your work.

You can do more with less if you give it enough thought and practice.

Studying Others Success

One of the best methods I have used to grow my business is by studying successful agents, and copying their behavior. Successful people from other professions can also provide inspiration for you to plan out your success and set ambitious goals. The reason is simple, what they are doing is working. There are a lot of great agents who provide video and written content on their success. This information can be found in interviews, training material, biographies, and self-help/business-improvement books and video. You can also go out to interview agents yourself, you can even write up the interview to post on a blog, or social media to share with others who may be interested.

Read about successful agents and follow them on social media, you will learn a lot by their example. Reading and studying about successful agents from the start, will help stimulate productive ideas, and motivate you to productive actions.

Through this kind of study, we can see how far a single agent can really go. We can learn about how they did it, and we can use that information to develop our own plan for success. By following their work ethic and learn what worked for them, new agents will have a head start on the path toward success. This kind of study should be constant. Read books and articles, watch video, and talk to successful agents to learn what you can. It is a business building activity that you should dedicate some time to every single day, right alongside mastering your presentations and prospecting.

Collaborate With A Mentor/Expert

Collaboration is just as important as observation. Whenever I meet with an agent with more experience or a higher production than me I pick their brain. This has been an unlimited source of delight for some, and not for others. You may join a company where you are paired with a mentor, or you will have the opportunity to meet with or call someone at any time to ask questions, talk about your plans, ask them how they run their business, etc. That is a truly amazing opportunity, and should be treasured. As a newer agent, the greatest gift for you and your livelihood is a guide and mentor to her you get started. When I meet with an agent that I want to learn from, I pull out my notebook or open my note taking app on my phone, and begin jotting things down. I turn casual conversations into something that looks like a journalist's interview. Usually that behavior is appreciated. I haven't met one agent who doesn't appreciate someone the attention, or who asked me to put the notes away.

To take things one step further, I recommend that newer agents talk to each other about their business, and about any issues they are dealing with. Collaborating throughout the learning experience will help the group learn more, faster, without each individual having to have the experiences on their own. Just as important is masterminding with experienced agents. Not only discussing problems on the horizon, it can be a great learning experience to approach mentors and ask any questions you may have. Most of them would be happy to help, for the agents who have no interest in collaboration, it is probably best to leave them in their own little world and move on to find someone who is interested and able to offer advice.

Should You Ever Change Plans?

We have been discussing goal setting and plans. A time will come when you will want to ask yourself if you have the right ones. That is normal, and anyone thinking about their plans and their future must wonder if they are truly taking the best actions, and focusing on the right goals. When you reach this point, the answer is maybe. If something is clearly not working, or you learn about a new prospecting activity that requires a change, but is superior, go for it. Always change plans for the better. Always adjust goals higher. You originally wanted to make $100k this year, but want to change it to $200 or $300? Go for it, upgrade your plan and take action accordingly. When it comes to a negative change, be careful. If you need to reduce your actions, reduce your goals, or take time away from your career, think twice before you act. You need to be sure that you have a significant reason to back down, and it can never be that you are just hitting a rough patch. If you persevere, you will overcome your obstacles.

Say you want to give up on your goal of closing three sales a month, and make your new goal to close only one a month. That decision is suspect because it lowers the bar and will not help you grow your business. You need to show that you have a powerful and irresistible want or need to reduce your target. You feel like you're working too hard and need more sleep? Maybe you are missing all of your favorite shows and important games, so you want some more TV time? That may be important to you, but it is not going to improve your life, it's going to take away from it. Working as hard as you can and making no apparent progress to your goals? It's just a sign that you need to increase your activity and/or shift your focus or your methods. Now, if you are working so much that your significant other is so unhappy you are putting your family in jeopardy, that is different. Maybe you have kids and you have been missing out on too much. Maybe your parents are sick and cannot live without your assistance. Those are compelling reasons to reduce your time working, but not your goals. Lets assume that you have a sick baby, and you literally cannot leave the house for most of the week. You know that you will not have enough time to make any appointments, and you know that without appointments, you have a recused chance of turning prospects into clients. Dont feel guilty if you had some setbacks, or weren't working your plan as well as you wanted. If you reach a point where you see that you are too far behind to catch up, don't fall into the trap of deciding to lower your target, and set a plan of action that matches what you are already doing. Molding your plans by matching them to your present behavior will be a waste of time. If you want to grow, you need to set ambitious goals with lots of productive action attached to them. If you take the unexpected down time and use it to work productively on smaller projects like improving your CMA's, listing presentations, scripts, updating notes, etc. I am certain that you can find some extra time here and there to help you get more efficient. If you can really hone your listing presentations and learn a more accurate method for selecting comparable properties and adjusting the numbers in your CMA, you should be able to improve your conversion rate and be able to set more competitive pricing on your listings. Buyers agents could use that time to implement home search systems or research neighborhoods for clients to help them find a home faster than before. You can squeeze every drop of productivity you have, so when the time comes to get fully back in action, you can pick up the pace so well that you may surpass even your original goals.

Build Your Business

Advertisements

There are few methods of building your brand and showing your face that are as wide reaching as advertisements. You have to pay to advertise, but if you can get featured in an article or be publicly recognized and have your information posted, you can get a free plug every now and then. Some companies will provide funds to pay for ads, and all of them will probably let you advertise on your own. As I have said before, you can spend all of your money on ads, and you may not make it all back right away, but a steady and consistent marketing plan will pay off over the course of your career.

Advertisements solve an important problem: obscurity. The only reason why you don't have clients beating down your door is because barely any people know you. If you have a thousand personal friends and acquaintances, what is the proportion of that network compared to the population of your entire city or county. I'm not diminishing the value of our personal network; I want to put this into perspective. It is likely that less than 1 in 1000 people in your market area know you or have heard of you. You want everyone to know you or know of you, and you want them all to go to you first when its time for them to buy or sell. The reality of the situation is that it is extremely difficult to reach every single person in your community. Advertisements help cover some ground, but they have to work in conjunction with your own mailings, blogs, articles, social media posts, videos, flyers, networking events, or whatever else you can put out into the world. Once people know you, they will go to you. Imagine if everyone in just your hometown considered you when they thought of real estate. Even in small towns, there are so many transactions a year that if only one or two agents owned them all they would be very rich indeed.

During my first year, I did not use paid adds until I realized that I was in trouble, and in desperate need of leads, and then I only used expensive internet lead services. My targeting was inconsistent and an unreliable number and quality of leads were barely trickling in. I also didn't realize until long afterwards that cold internet leads took the longest to convert (sometimes 12 months or more), and were the most difficult of all to work with. It takes time for online ads, and purchased leads to pay off. If someone hears about me today, but isn't ready to buy until next year, they may have liked what they heard or saw, but what are the odds that when the time comes, they remember your name and number? There needs to be a system already in place for long term nurturing, and there needs to be a lot of great, even compelling content to keep that audience engaged.

A new agent starting out needs to use highly targeted ads, and they need to be special. If you are a new agent and you think sending out 500 cards to a demographic every month, or every week, how are your conversion rates going to be compared to a company with 1,000 times your budget that has been around for 25 years? You will essentially be wasting your money. But if you were to choose 100 addresses of expired or cancelled listings, and specially tailor your message to that group, you are more likely to get a response. Better yet, if you are farming a small group, you can personalize the mailers and letters, you can even send them market reports and updates. Put more time into research and think about what will make you stand out the most. Try to follow up cards and letters with phone calls and emails too. It is better to find a small group that you know wants to buy or sell and really work hard on showing them who you are, than to throw mud at the wall and hope that you randomly caught someone at the right moment.

Want to stand out on a budget? Find interesting things that no one else is doing, use them to customize or create marketing material, and I make a much stronger impression. You can make interesting crafts, you could set up an arrangement with local businesses to offer discounts to your customers, or even "free" treats that you would pay for later if they redeem a coupon or a postcard with the promotion on it (think cupcakes, ice-cream, and other goodies to promote during different seasons and holidays. There are ton's of great ideas online to advertise yourself. Target only people who are in your sphere of influence, so your marketing can be highly targeted, and cost-effective. After you build your business and people begin to learn about you, you can take a step back and target larger areas, but in the beginning you have to start small to build a strong foundation to your business.

Referral Business

There is no business like repeat and referral business. Your strongest source of leads will be from your network, and your network's network. This includes past clients, and other real estate professionals. Sometimes you know a lot of people who are not ready to move right now. However, they may have some connections to someone that is ready to move. Some agents don't like to ask their friends and family for business for various reasons. No matter how you feel about it, you should ask for business, and you should prospect in your personal network like you would anywhere else. Tell everyone you know that you are an agent, and tell them that you are looking for business. People have to know you and what you do in order to even consider working with you. You are in a sales job, and your customers are everyone. The only way to gain inventory and close sales is by first generating leads. Before you are in the real sales estate business, you are in the lead generating business.

By far the easiest source of leads is through your network. You already know them, they know you, and they probably like you too. You have a group of people that will be happy to work with you as an agent, in fact most of them would probably prefer to work with someone they know. I have encountered many people who did not want to work with an agent in their network because they "don't want to mix business with family." The family/business problem is understandable, and if you come across a family member who thinks this, tell them:

"I will do a better job than someone else because they know and I care about your, and you know that I will be able to find you a great deal. Another agent may only be in it for the paycheck, and doesn't know you or your needs as well. Who is going to bring all of their energy and genuinely care more about their friends getting the best deal? Some other agent? They won't have that level of a commitment."

If this person responds that they would love to work with you, but they want to work with an agent with more experience, or who has sold more property before, that is when you leverage your mentor and your offices experience. You can tell them that your office has sold x properties in the last month or year, and it was a total of $X in sales volume. Tell them that you are working with an experienced agent who is going to bring an additional x years of experience to the table, and who will help you get the property sold. Ask this person, "would you be able to get a better deal if I brought you over 100 combined years of real estate sales experience, and gave you access to...." that is where you bring in your value proposition. Establishing yourself as an expert, and as the best agent to help them is easy when you understand how to articulate your value, and will help you capture that referral personal sphere of influence, and referral business. On the flip side, this can put agents in an awkward position when they meet with a client who has a friend or family member who is an agent and this client explains their desire to avoid the family/business problem. If you meet them, always try to take the business, tell them that you understand their decision, and move on with the deal. If a prospect indicates that they know an agent, but have already chosen not to use them, don't insist that they call that agent up. It is your duty as the agent to work with your network, and if you don't, someone else will.

Your friends and family will all need a real estate agent at some point in their lives, and it is up to you to be there when they need you. If you choose not to, that's fine, but the deal will still happen without you, and someone else will take the commission. One day you might find someone close to you is under contract or had just closed a deal, and they just plain forgot that you were an agent, or they didn't realize that you would be able to help them. It happens when you aren't following up enough, or if you aren't making it clear that you can work with them in whatever market they are in. It is also a testament that no agent, new or experienced, is immune from the necessity to constantly be marketing and generating leads. If you want to take all of the business that you possibly can, you need to look and ask for it. If you maintain your presence in the market and in your network's mind, you will get referrals, and you will get repeat deals. You will sell a house to your cousin who tells their friends about you, you will help them buy a house, then over the years your cousin will need to move, and use you again to sell and buy anew. Over the years you can build up such a network that more than half of your business is through repeat and referral clients. I have met agents who have almost only been working with repeats and referrals. It is a powerful and potentially unlimited resource if treated properly, and as a newer agent it is your most important source of leads for your first deals.

Follow-Up

Repeat and referral business can be an extremely strong source of leads. The purpose of follow up is to keep you on their minds when they think of real estate. If they already like you and think that you are a great agent, then don't let them forget about you. Being forgotten can be a new agent's most expensive mistake, do not let it happen. If they are past clients, thank them for the business and offer them something thoughtful in return for working with you. I have sent things like pens, calendars, books, etc. I know of agents that send seasonal decorations like wreaths and flowers. The exact use and nature of the gift does not matter past the point of the recipients appreciation of it. It needs to be something that they will use or keep. Then send them a calendar every year or a nice letter, or if you are creative, make something special. Let your past clients know that you care about them, and that you were very glad to have done business with them. Occasionally check in to see if they or their friends need an agent, and that you prefer to work with referral leads because it is your favorite source of business. This will keep you in the front of their mind whenever they think of buying or selling a home, and when the inevitable "hey, do you know a good agent?" question will be asked, whose name will they give? Your past client from five years ago may be ready to move again, or their friends or family are looking to buy their first home. You can't give once and expect them to remember you for the rest of their lives. Follow up periodically over the years, how often depends on you, but at a minimum it should be something every year. The initial gifts are important in selection, but they do not need to be overly expensive. The followup plan needs to be long term, but it does not need to be on a weekly basis.

As a newer agent your foremost concern will be controlling your costs while growing your business. There are some services that are relatively cheap, and work well for the long term follow up. For example, some companies provide the option to pay around $40 or $50 to choose a 3 year follow up plan, with seasonal cards, birthday cards, yearly calendars with your face all over them, others offer different variations of this, and some even have a magazine subscription. Tools like those are indeed powerful, but I know that similar programs can be manually designed for less. All a new agent needs is a calendar with recurring events or a spreadsheet with dates and lists of touch points. You can make 12, 20, 30 touch programs, really any number would be appropriate. I limit my touch points to a minimum of 12, but not more than 30. I don't want my client to forget me, but sending a mailer a week would be very taxing for both of us. I use the softer follow up plans on clients who I know very well and know that they won't forget me because I'll see them in person periodically. For past clients that I may never speak to again, I make sure to send them the maximum number of gifts, cards, and to build a strong enough mindshare. Leaving a good first impression is important, but nothing shows people how valuable you are like a good long term contact through thoughtful gifts, cards, mailers, phone calls, emails, etc.

Networking

Networking can change your life. Meeting that one person who can connect you with all of the business that you desire can step your business up to the next level instantly. For some this boost will come with current or past clients, their company, or meeting new people in the community through joining groups or volunteering. A new agent needs to get out there, because no one can work with an agent they don't know, and no one knows the newest agent's. Unless you are beginning your career as a celebrity, you don't know enough people. You will need to go out and make yourself known. Your network, or your sphere of influence will be your strongest source of leads as yo are building your business. Grow your network, and you will earn more. Giving back to the community, volunteering, gifting, all of these methods help to grow your network in active and passive forms. Paid advertising, asking people you know for referrals, and joining local clubs and other organizations are all activities that will help establish yourself as an agent in the community. You will be able to stand out from your competition by being more familiar to those people you interact with. Every time you show your face, your name, and your brand, you are steadily building your network.

Some people will talk about networking in ways that make it seem like only business events and seminars are where it happens. All social gatherings are for networking. Any interaction that you are a part of that gets someone thinking or talking about you is networking. Those agents with massive networks eventually find that people will seek them out, or they find that many people they meet have already herd of or seen them. A new agent's networking goal should be to develop a sphere of influence that eventually brings in unsolicited business. Getting to that point is not as difficult as it may seem. It's mostly time consuming. You grow your network one relationship at a time. Your network is simply your personal connections. You can make those connections in person or remotely. Phone, and internet networking works, but is less effective than in person. Meeting with people face-to-face is much more memorable, and the people you meet can engage with you better. Going out and meeting people is a business building activity. Making connections can lead to buyer or listing appointments, appointments lead to signed contracts, which leads to listings and active buyers, until they ultimately end in closings. Try to meet new people and talk about real estate every day.

CRM

Customer Relationship Management (CRM) systems come in many shapes and sizes. It is a program that stores your contacts, and it helps track your interactions with them. There are industry specific CRM's, there are general ones, and you could even make your own on a spreadsheet. You can even find some that integrate with lead generating websites, where you use paid advertisements to drive traffic to the real estate site, get people to sign up or request showings, and when they do sign up, they are immediately dropped into the CRM with a followup plan attached to them as a new lead. There are so many software companies working on these programs, that cheap functional CRM software should not be hard to find. There you could call, email, or research into what listings they were looking at, and update notes. I can also put those leads on email alerts, follow up plans, etc. and you could look at their search history and viewed listings through the site.

My first year I did not use any industry specific technology except for the Multiple Listing Service (MLS). I had begun working on a website at the end, but it was awful. When it came to contacts, I just saved them in my phone. I made sure to put "buyer lead," "seller lead," listing agent for 12 main st," etc in there as well. That system worked perfectly until I had about 10 new contacts to track, and I had to waste time remembering who was who, and what I needed to talk to them about. To augment this I began taking notes on paper, and it served only to further complicate an inefficient system. After a year of work and contacts, I have met many people whom I could not remember from only saving a few reminder words next to their name. If I had some notes on their contact file, maybe a photo, maybe even some information on my last conversations with them, I would have been better off. You will be able to get by without any real organization when you only have a few contacts. What is your plan when you have over a hundred, or thousand? Are you going to remember who is a lead that's not ready to buy for a couple of years, who is ready now, and which ones are just agents and vendors you have done business with? If you dont capture and organize all of this information, in a very short period of time you will loose track of people. The chaos will be overwhelming, and even if you can muster a burst of mental energy to try and power through it, it will quickly fizzle out. You will need to use a CRM program, a spreadsheet, or even flashcards, just keep the information as it comes, and keep it organized in an accessible way. Almost all agents will leverage technology for this task. Select a program that at a minimum can store your contacts, notes for each one, date of last contact, and offer reminders for people or contacts that you haven't reached out to in a while. That is the minimum. You can use a program that links to your website, sends automatic emails and uses follow up plans, or does even more for you. After you build up a good contact database, you can farm it for more leads. Many agents get a constant trickle of business year after year from their past clients, and even referrals from brokers or agents that they have worked with before. The only way to track a large database is with specially designed software.

Find a cheap or even free CRM. Your company may provide one, you may be able to get one at a discount, or if you don't have a lot of capital, start on a spreadsheet like Apple Numbers, Google Sheets, or Microsoft Excel. Get the lowest cost option for the best desired result. You don't need a system that a large company will use, and you don't want to use a paper book or your phone contacts list alone. With the right system you can keep track of everyone and everything. Once you get your CRM up and running put in leads that are given to you, also put in your personal contacts too anyone you have ever known should go in there. Build your prospecting lists, and start making business calls. You will not just earn new business, you will have peace of mind knowing that you have a reliable system in place to remind you of who you need to call next.

Work Every Day

As an agent, you need to work every day, though we all strive to achieve that precious less-work/more-life balance. I even have trouble with it. Now let's define work. As an agent, your work is closing, or taking any thought or action to reach that end. So calls, texts, emails (if you are trying to close a deal or get a lead to close, etc) are work. Filling and filing forms, filing paperwork, and faxing is work. Making appointments and meeting people is work. Writing and reading is work. Talking and eating is work. Just thinking about your business, really anything can be work

A lot of us get caught up thinking that we shouldnt have to work too hard, or too much. The reason why so many agents have that too-much-work/not-enough-life balancing problem is because there is a gray line separating the two activities. Think about it. What if your friend calls to ask about your weekend plans and mentions that the house up the street from him is on the market. You talk about it, and the market in his town. Are you working? Then your friend wonders what he could sell his house for, he has always wanted to live closer to the lake, or center of town, or wherever. You begin to talk about what his home's value may be, or the importance of pre-approval and planning before he puts his house on the market. Are you working now? Then he asks if you could figure out what it will sell for and talk about it when you visit that weekend. Now you are definitely working, right? You will have clearly defined activity that is well away from that wall of separation, but once you get close, the massive wall of separation looks more like a short decorative wall, something easy to step over. When you are on it, it may be hard to tell it's there at all. That is why it is so important to work every day. It's difficult to draw the line, and it's so easy to answer some email and make a quick call. I don't think that everyone should put in a set number of hours, or work hard all day every day. Some agents do need to keep a few days sacred, and most people need a vacation every now and then.

What needs to be avoided at all costs is the feeling of being overwhelmed with all of the things that can and should be done, then taking no action whatsoever. What follows non-action is a scenario where there becomes so much to do, it becomes difficult to even figure out where to start.

I say work every day, no matter how big or small the task may be. Lot's of new agents, even professionals in other industries, are constantly worried about becoming slaves to their phones and never getting time with their families. Family time, and other important moments need to take precedence over anything else. You can work every day without a huge time commitment by filling in those odd few minutes we all get throughout the day on a weekend or a holiday. I check and respond to email that only need a short reply, anything more involved I defer to dedicated processing time. An email takes seconds to type, and sometimes I'll add a note or task in my calendar to go along with it as well. It's so quick and easy, I get to feel a little productive no matter where I am, or what I am doing. I'll occasionally take calls off hours as well on deals in progress, but I usually just take the message if it's not important. I check my CRM every morning, no matter what, and if I have been out of touch with someone for a while, I'll send a quick email and make a note in my calendar to call them the next business day. That's about all that I do when I'm giving myself time off. It will take 5-10 minutes throughout a day. If I catch a huge issue that needs to be dealt with right then, I will. In fact, it is more of a relief than a bother to stay on top of all of my obligations instead of playing catch up afterwards.

Listings

There are a few key skills that need special attention in growing your business. The top two would be generating leads, and getting listings. We have gone over lead generation, but let's now give special attention to the listings. When it comes to growing your business, listings are the name of the game. Listings property is a high-leverage, low-effort activity that can grow your business faster than anything else. An agent can have many listings at one time, with no real loss of service quality. However, an agent cannot realistically have very many active buyers without soon feeling overworked and in need of help. Buyers are essential to the industry's continued operation, but they are time intensive. I can have 10+ listings at a time, run open houses, distribute marketing mailers and other ads, accept offers and negotiate to sell, all without skipping a beat. If I had 10 active buyers who wanted to go on showings, make offers, and take trips through favored neighborhoods all at the same time, I would be in trouble. Sometimes as a newer agent it is easier to work with buyers first. It's normal to have a hard time picking up listings at first, and working with buyers is a great way to learn the business. When it is time to pick things up a notch, you want to focus on listings. You will first need listing leads. Those leads can be had initially from your personal network. Next, you can look to company generated leads if they can provide some. Then you can farm for expired, cancelled, and FSBO leads. Those generation methods are cheap or free, depending on how you do it. You can build a sizable list over time. You can almost never truly exhaust those sources. If you are enjoying some success and have established yourself, you can buy leads or hire someone to work on lead generation for you. Until then, you are your one and only lead generator.

When To Expand

The ultimate purpose of a business should be to grow. A business that doesn't grow, is like a truck spinning its wheels, stuck in the mud. It's making a lot of noise, its throwing dirt, and looks like a lot of activity is going on, but it's not moving. As an agent you are running a business. You are your boss, and your business' success is solely dependent on you. Expansion should be on your mind. There will be times when you feel like you're stuck in the mud no matter what you do, but even the deepest quagmire will dry up in the right conditions. Sometimes you just need time, sometimes you need a new approach. If you keep up the good work, you will grow your sales. At some point, your business will grow to a point where you will be ready to take it to the next level. This exact point is is relative, no two agents will reach it at the same time (but they should reach it). Usually that point is about money. When you have enough income that allows for investment in your business, that is what you should do. Too many productive agents increase their expenses proportionally to their income. If you can maintain your present costs of living, or even tighten your budget while reinvesting in your business' expansion, you will be far ahead of your peers.

Any agent starting out fresh is in a tentative time. The first few deals may be difficult, they may be easy, but it will be stressful. You will be in that slump of worry, but once you push through, you will come out with a little cash, and even more valuable experience. Your first expansion should be in lead generation. Don't worry about all of the technical things right away, although you should be learning about your company and about getting a website, CRM, designing mailers, etc. Your first big move needs to be for generating more leads, and then more business. This can be aided by adding on an auto-dialing service to make more contacts, more marketing material, more mailings, adding on a website for lead generation and targeted advertisements. With growing numbers of leads and the increase in business, you will need a larger infrastructure, but not until after your business grows. You gain some business, expand a little, gain some more, then expand some more. If your personal expenses outgrow your business income, you will overspend and go down the broke-agent path. If you focus only on your work, and the things you need to help you work, you will be in a much better position. Growing properly should see you transitioning to better technology and equipment over time. Those advances should be taken as baby steps on an as-needed basis. If you try to move too quickly, you could become unstable, and easily toppled over. If you take incremental baby steps, maintaining a strong and stable foundation so that nothing could throw you off course, it will pay off very well in the long run. If you are constantly growing with your business, and you are always working on closing more deals, you will be always taking those expansive steps. Guard against premature expenses. Don't buy a marketing program now that you will have to cancel in a few months because you didn't get an instant return.

Going Above And Beyond

I have touched on this periodically, but the point cannot be over stressed. Going above and beyond the minimum requirements for any action will yield massive results. Many people are energized at the start, but quickly burn out and lose interest. This burnout is a side effect of hard work without results. We start with excitement and lots of energy, everything is new and exciting. We hit the ground running, we take massive actions, we work hard, and then nothing happens, or the results don't match the effort. This point is critical, because it is not a sign that you just can't get it right, or that you aren't a good agent. That point is a sign that your energy and activity is right, but you need to shift your focus, or change your actions in some way, results are feedback. It doesn't matter what the activity is. It could be work, it could be assembling Ikea furniture, it could be writing your novel, yard work, painting, re-decorating, it doesn't matter. The going got tough as a sign that you can change your actions, of that you aren't taking enough action. As an agent you will notice that there are many brokerages and many agents working in every community. You will also see that there are even more homes being bought and sold than there are agents working. It may be more or less difficult to break into a particular market, but in the end the most productive agents are taking the most productive actions. If this is your first job, your first career, part time, full time, or this is a new move after years in another industry, you can still make a great living if you generate leads, convert them to clients, and close sales. As a newer or inexperienced agent, your greatest asset will be your ability to outwork the competition. If you can outwork them, you can outperform them, and soon enough you will make a name for yourself as an outstanding agent. Your career will explode. You can go from being a no-name agent to a top producer in a very short time.

One of the best ways to learn is to get immediate negative feedback from an action. Its what you learn from your results that will help you succeed. When you notice an area that needs improvement, make a note of it, analyze how you can do it better next time, talk to another agent about it, make some more notes, and go out and try again. Instead of mistakes and failures, you now have learning experiences. Because in reality, the only tome you have failed, is when you stop. now have learning experiences. Along with that, no matter how badly a day may be going for me, I remember the feeling of successfully executing a contract, negotiating for my clients, and closing a deal. I want my buyers to get the biggest discounts, I want my sellers to get top dollar for their houses. I want a fast and smooth deal that is a win-win for all parties to the transaction. I use that desire to fuel my activity. Honestly, making those deal's happen is fun. It amazes me to think that I can help people get what they want, and make a good living at it. Real estate can be satisfying and enjoyable for you too, it should be fun for you. It will be fun for you if you do what it takes to be great, and go above and beyond the normal expectations for average agents.

Education

Why It's Important

Your real estate education is essential to any degree of success. If you don't know how to do your job, you obviously won't go very far. In order to learn how to complete your day to day tasks and drive your business, you need to have a real estate education. There are some colleges and universities that offer degree programs in real estate. If you are at a place in life where you are planning to go to college anyway, a real estate focused degree is a great option. If you are not there, and do not plan on going back to school, that's fine. You can do it by reading, writing, listening, observing, and hands-on experience. Luckily, most education can be had anywhere (home, office). Your systematic instruction can be entirely self-driven. You can make reading and listening to audio programs a new part of your daily routine. You can carry a notebook to take down important information and help you develop or capture new ideas. You can set time to sit down with a mentor and go over your presentation, or cover any questions you may have. You can even go through your material alone and take notes on your own thoughts, you can change your social media feeds and follow real estate based blogs. You can join real estate focused groups or meet ups where you know knowledgeable agents are populating (like landlord associations, Realtor associations, B.N.I. groups, etc.). You will need to learn all that you can, and there is no single greatest source of information, nor should you limit yourself to one source.

Don't Only Focus On real estate

Continuing education, as we already know, is important to your business. There is plenty of industry specific material. You can learn about sales in general to help you with your personal interactions and other aspects of sales like time management, lead follow up etc. You can learn about marketing and advertising. You can study social networks and learn how to maximize their potential. You can join writers' workshops. You can take classes on how homes are built, or how to work on do-it-yourself (DIY) home improvement projects. There is so much information in so many shapes and sizes, you should be able to find new information or a new perspective on what you already know forever.

The place to begin is by learning what you can and cannot do well. For example, how to make presentations, how to do the paperwork, how to negotiate, how the whole process works from start to end. Then as you are getting the gist of it, see where you need to improve. If you are a weak negotiator, look to industry specific material first. Read up on negotiating as it applies to agents, talk to a mentor, take some notes on how you are doing it, and what may be going wrong. Then you start getting into strategy, persuasion, and other periphery fields that apply. You always start narrow, then dig deep. Never start on a broad subject and think that you are going to go very deeply on "lead generation" before you narrow your focus to internet, expired, cancelled or for sale by owner listings, referrals, mailers, or any other methods of lead generation. You can start with introductory overviews to familiarize yourself with everything quickly, but you will want to master that one task by exploring into other industries and not only real estate specific material on very specific things.

The most important lesson from my first year is that if you want to change something, you need to take action. You need to read, talk, listen, think, and do. Just hoping something will change but doing nothing to facilitate that change is akin to not wanting it in the first place. What all new agents want is to be productive and make money. Maybe it is to feed a lifestyle you are accustomed to or want to have. Maybe you want to be an agent because you think it will be fun and exciting. Maybe you want to be an agent because you want to take charge of your life. Maybe you were like me, and got your license because it looked like the fastest and easiest way to make a fortune. Your motivation doesn't matter as much as your results and the actions you took to get them. If you are going to work, you may as well do the best you possibly can and hold yourself to the highest standards possible. Doing something just to barely get by is demoralizing and underproductive. You need to grow and learn as much as possible so you can become a master of your trade. You can become a master, but you need to learn. Learn about your work in general, specifically target weaknesses, then learn everything that there is to know about it, in real estate and even other industries.

Conclusion

How Much You Will Build On That First Year

Going forward, you will find that your first year sets a foundation for all of the years to come. If you have never been self managed before, and if you have never worked in sales before, the experience is going to be intense. The volume of information that you learn at the beginning can be overwhelming at times, but it can be dealt with in tiny chunks, one step at a time. Take notes to track your progress and identify weakly performing activities that you can focus on improving. You are going to learn so much every day, you won't even realize it. Those first years are where you build your foundation, and you want it to be solid. After you build your foundation of productive and successful habits, it will be easier to take on more business and more responsibility. The first year is the most important, not because you will make the most or least money, it's because you are going to learn the most. Your learning curve will be at its steepest, the volume of information you are taking in will be the highest. You will be developing all of the needed skills to thrive. After that first push, it won't be as easy to change unproductive behavior or habits that may end up costing you in the long run. Start on the right track, and hit the ground running. Commit yourself to making high goals and take massive actions. You will be building your brand, building your business, and building yourself all at once.

Take Action

If you have not yet gotten your license or weren't sure if becoming an agent is right for you, I hope that you have enough information now to take the leap and dive in. This work is easy to start, but it's not easy to excel in. Like any other industry, or any other profession, you will have to put the time in to learn. Unlike many other career paths, real estate is a pure meritocracy. The only money you earn is directly through your work. This means that you need to have a level of discipline that you may not be used to. If you have taken the knowledge I am giving you here, you now have the essential information to get started. You are already a world ahead of everyone else who never even bothered to pick up a book or audio program in the beginning. If you are licensed and have just broken into your market for the first time, or if you have been licensed for a time and are looking for some fresh ideas, I hope that I have given you some great take aways that will help you to go out and earn that extra business that you were looking for.

Whenever I finish a new book, I look forward to the next one, and the next bit of knowledge that I can take in to help me grow more and do better. Before I move on I think about what I have just been reading and thinking about for the past few days and hours. Sometimes I will just take information, and move on, sometimes I will learn something that will help me to take new actions too. My intention here was to give you both. I want you to have new information to think about going forward that will help your business, and I want to give you ideas of what actions to take. I know how hard it can be when you are just starting out. Even if you have been licensed for a whole year and haven't had any business. Even if it's been three years, you're doing OK, but you want to take it to the next level. The only way to have new results is through new actions. You can think about anything and everything. You can make plans and set goals all day, but those are all only tools to help you stay focused, and take action. You are probably going to have your own failures and mistakes, hopefully none as bad as mine. No matter what though, never give up, and never stop taking action.